contact: l.n.McBridedesigns@gmail.com

IBSN: 978-0-692-08049-8

Simple illustrations For colorful Expressions!

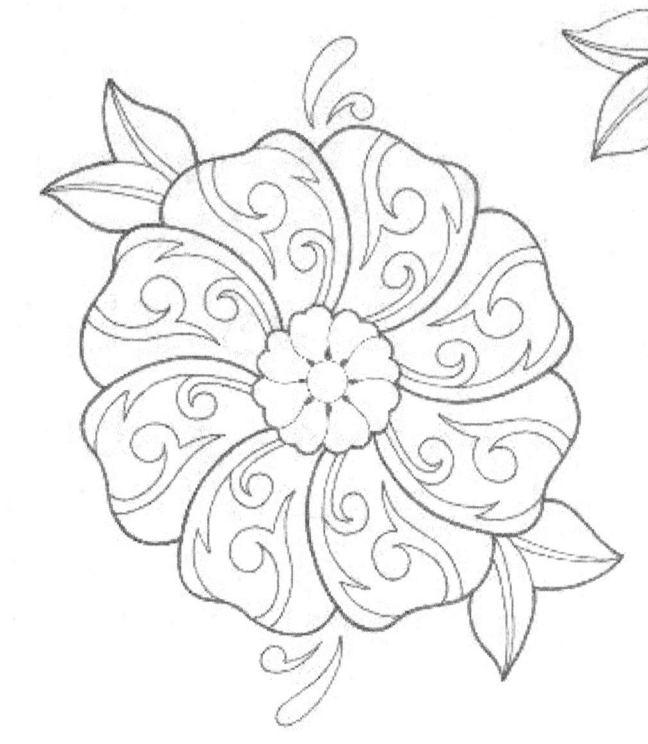

Dear colorist,

I'm so very proud to share this little labor of love with you, and I hope you find as much excitement and joy in the creative coloring process as I did in the creation of this book.

The coloring process is what helps brings these images to life.

The main ideas are here, but it its up to you to finish it.

Give it a strong presence of your personality.

Sincerely

Lacie McBride

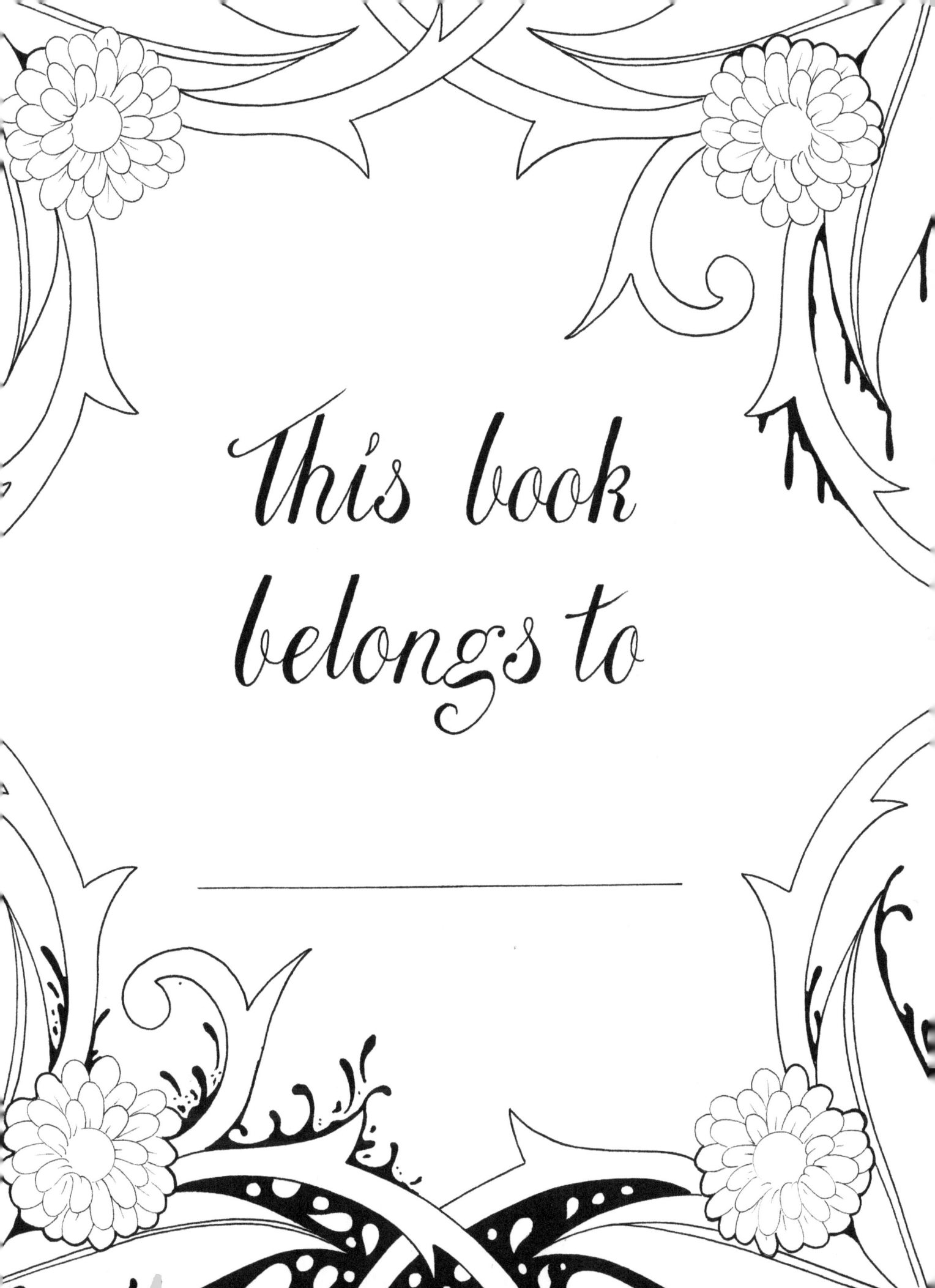

This book
belongs to

_____

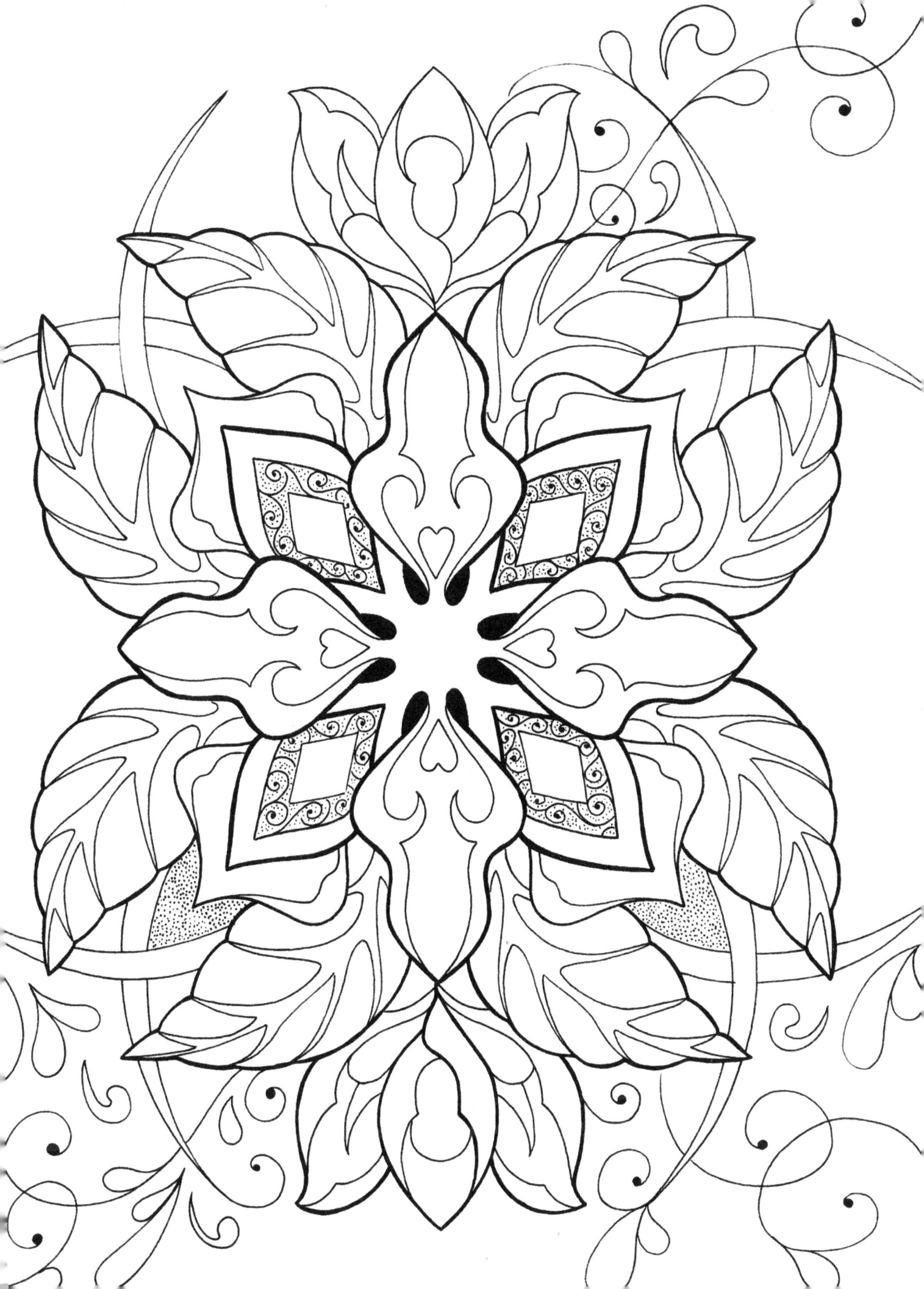

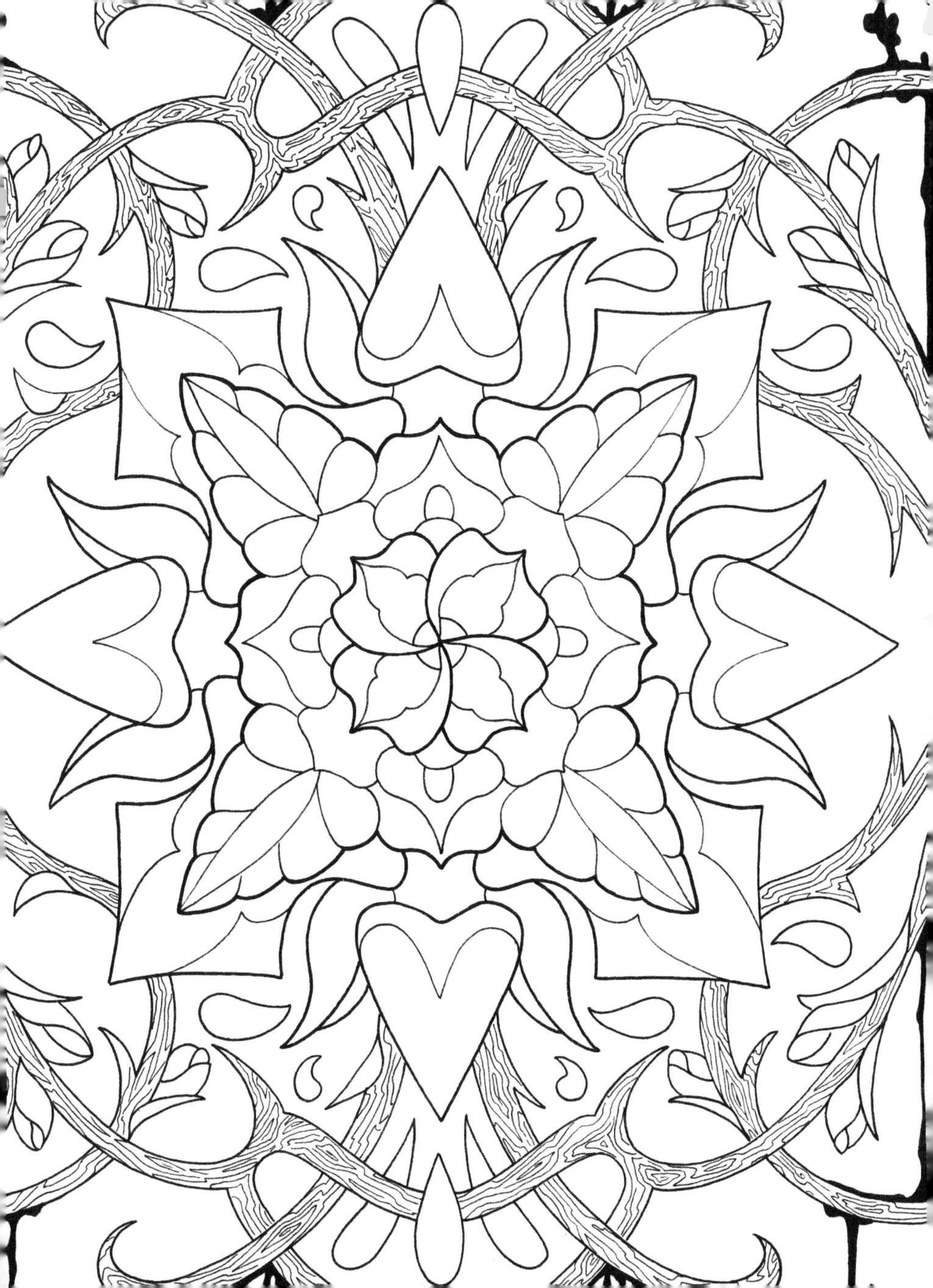

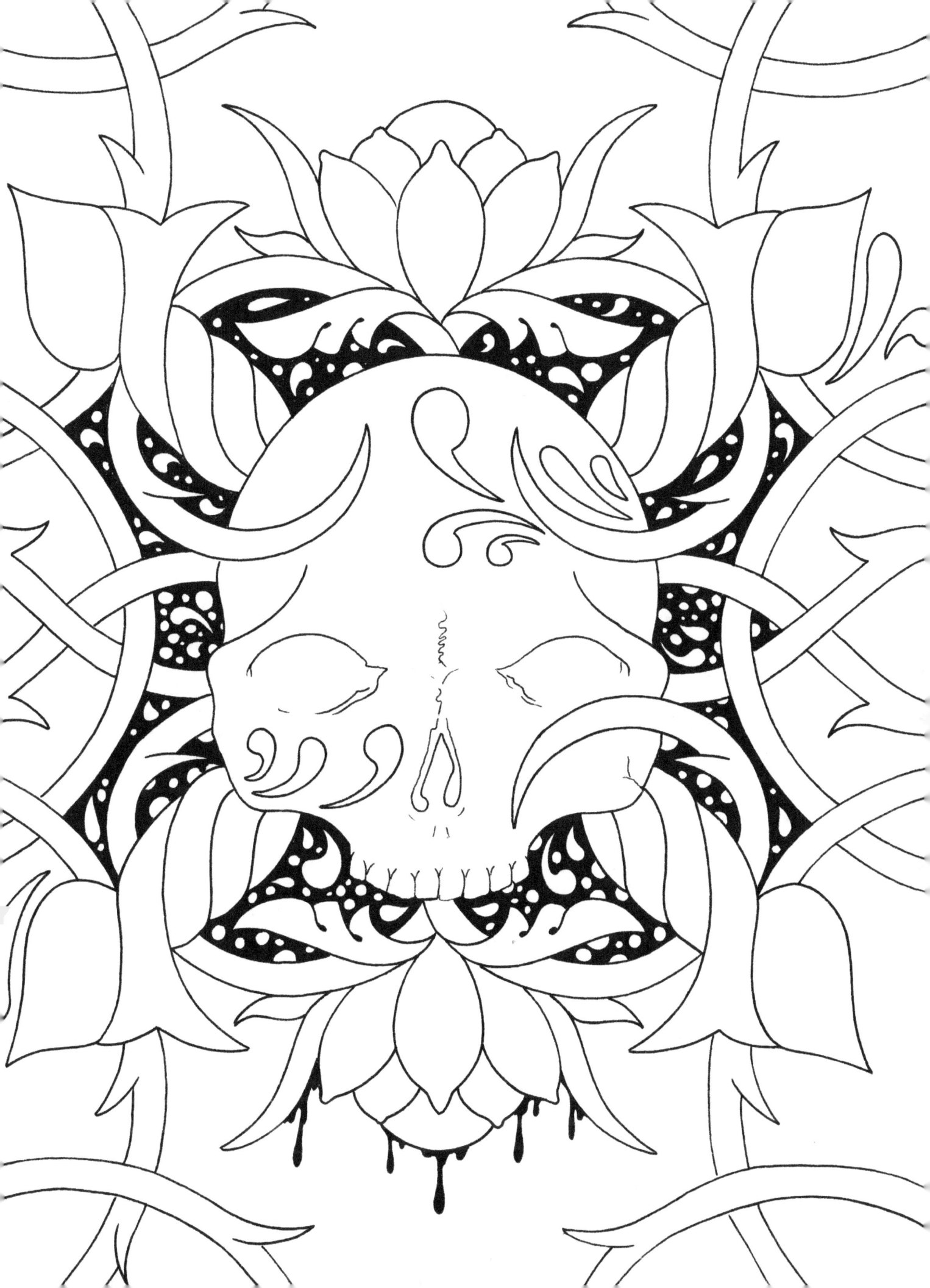

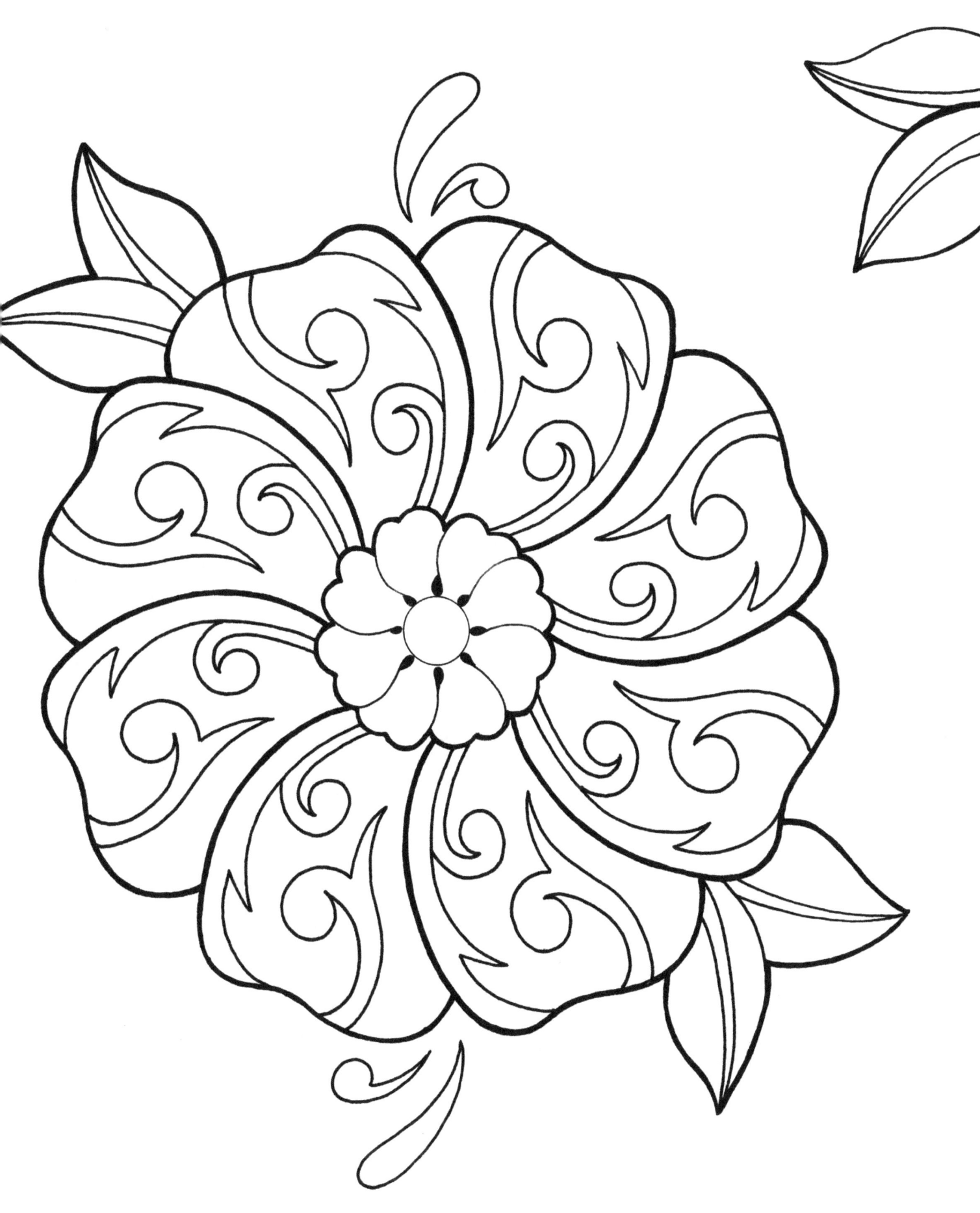

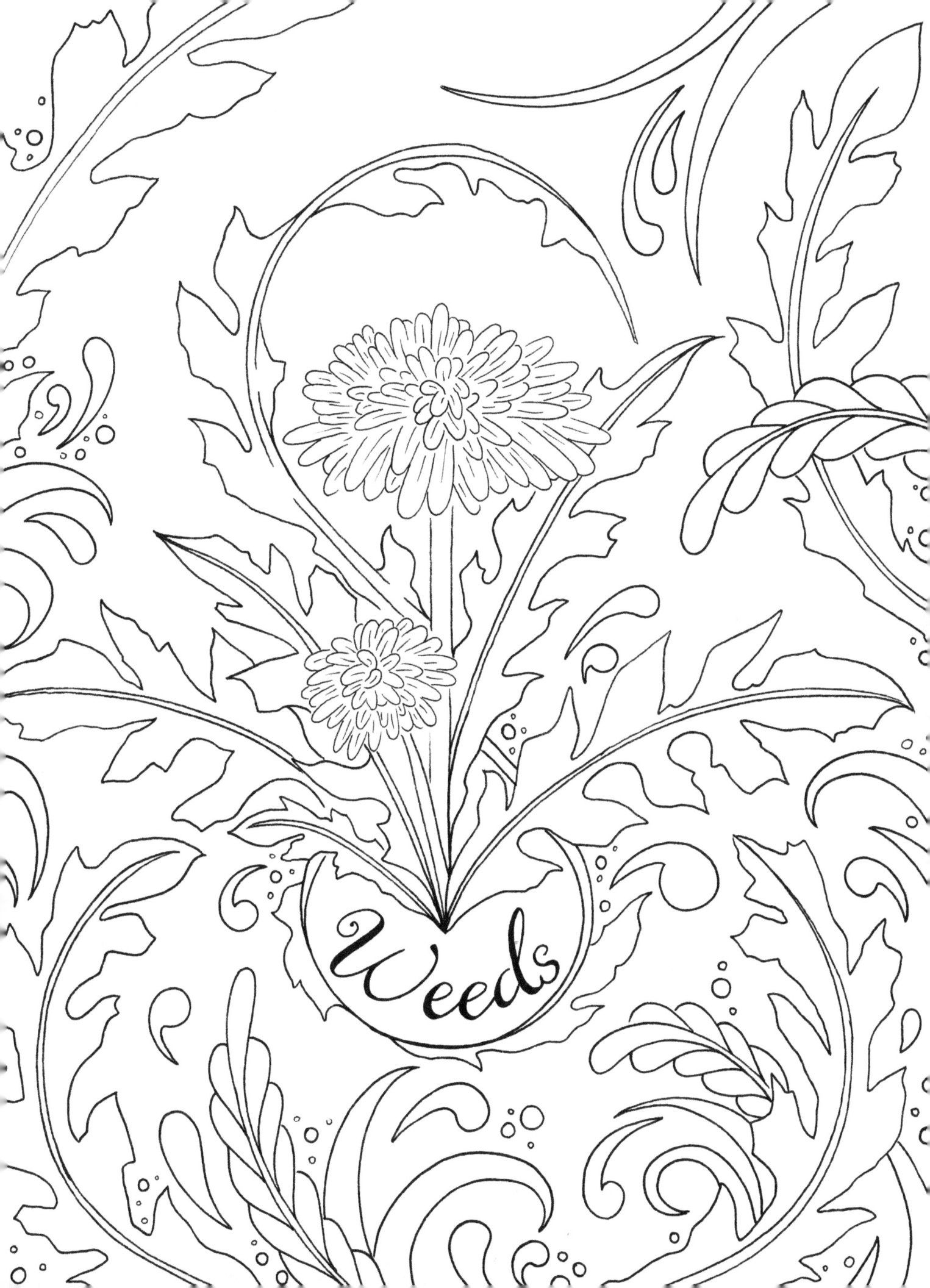

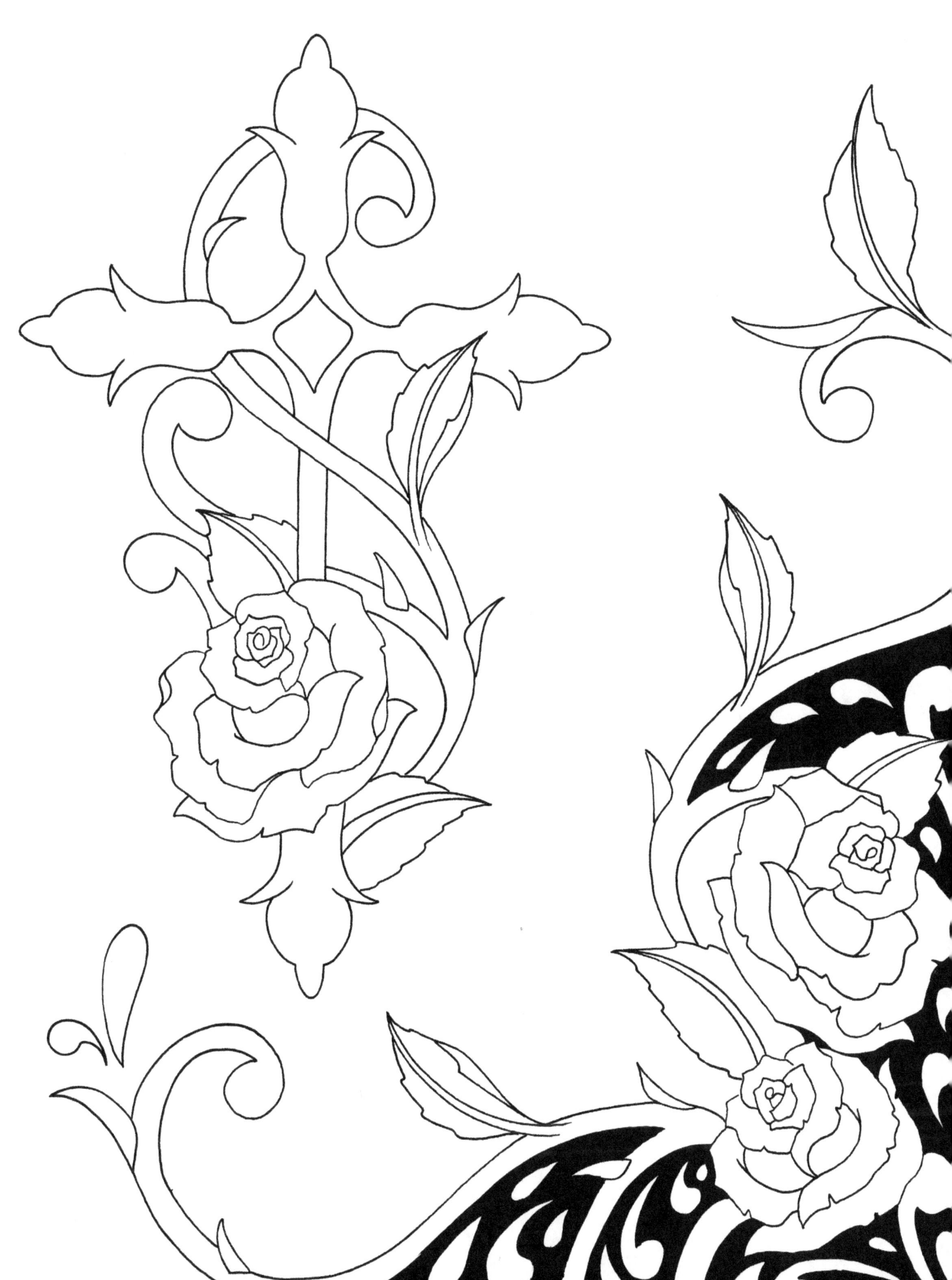

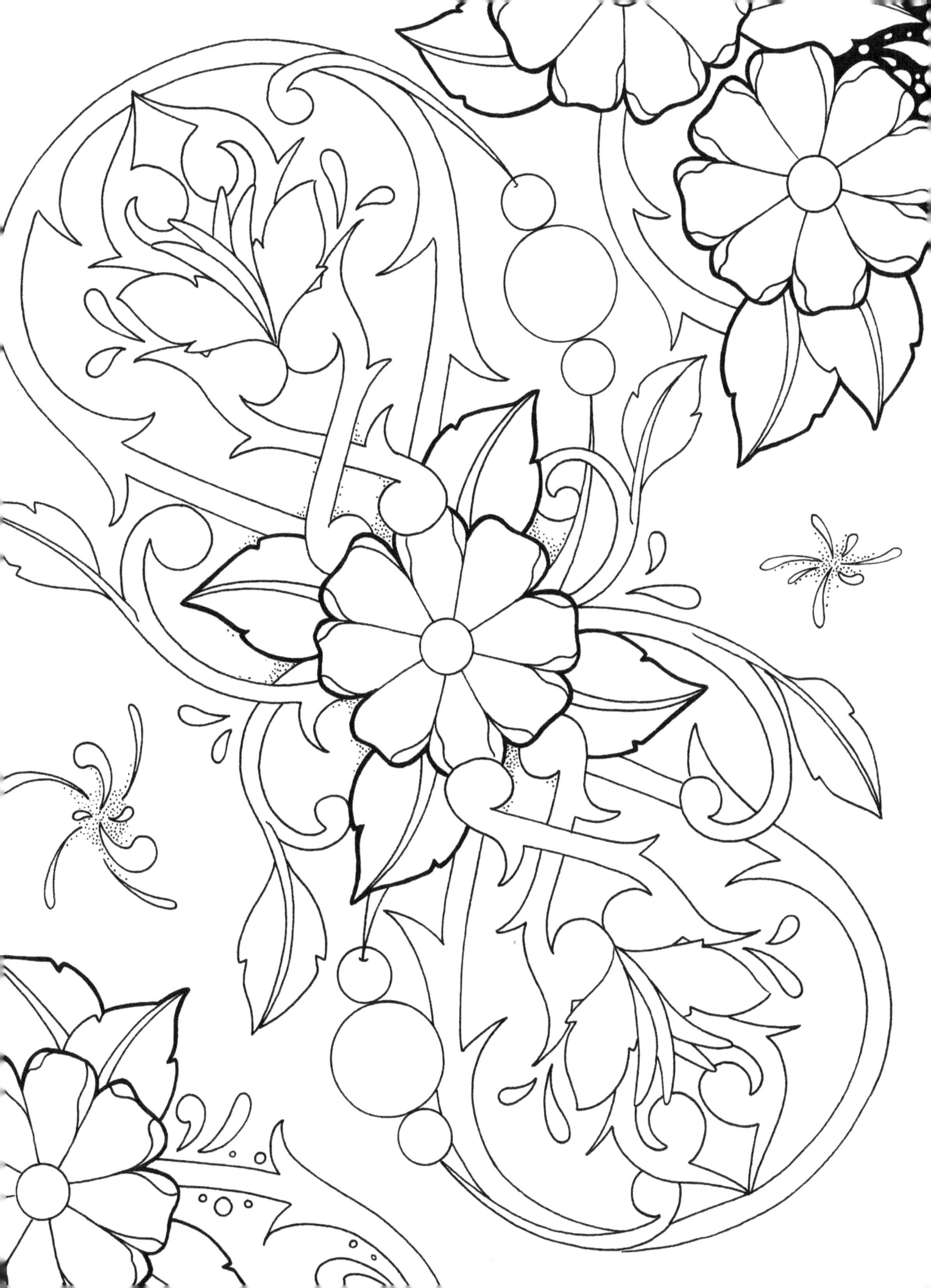

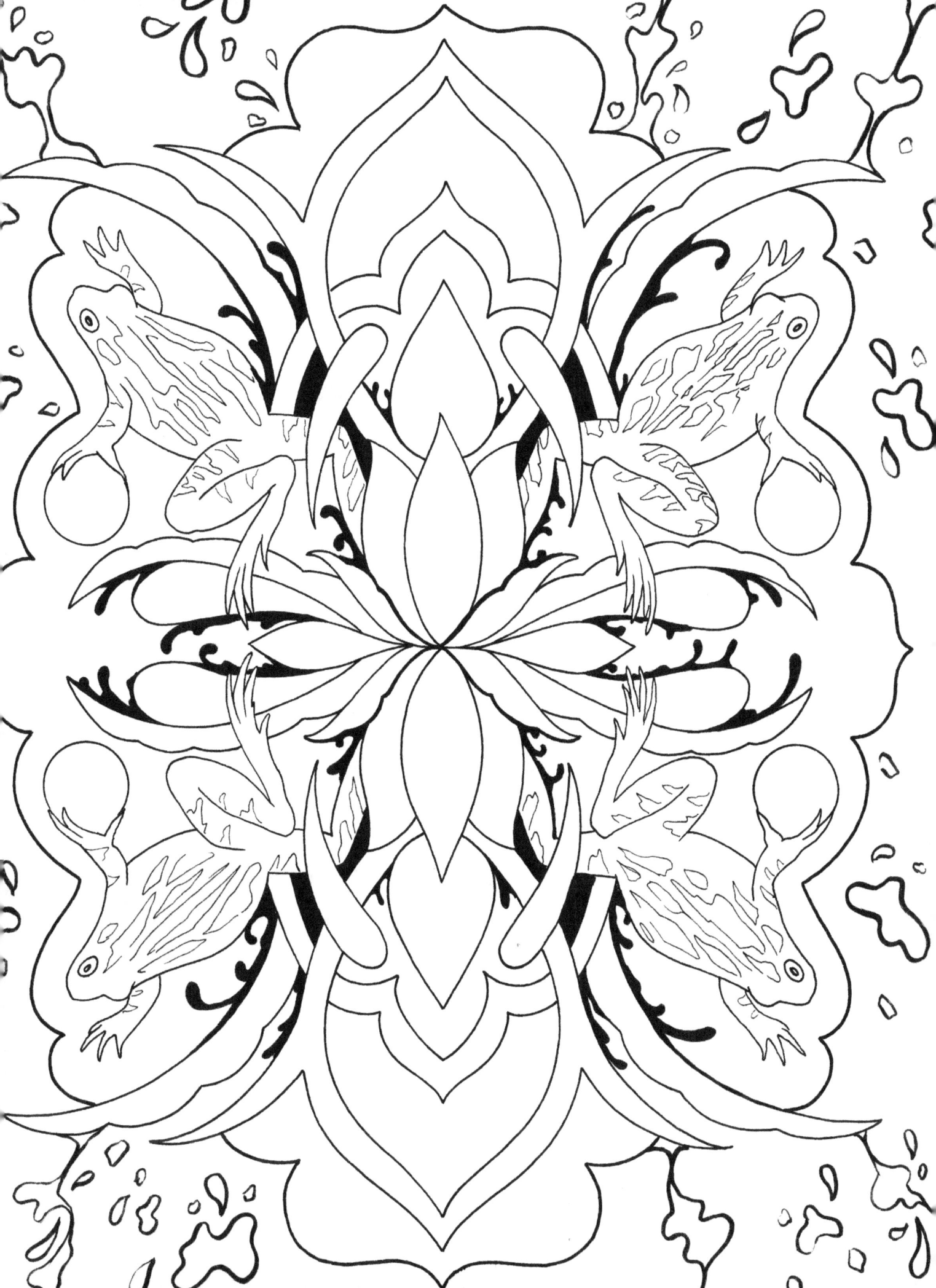

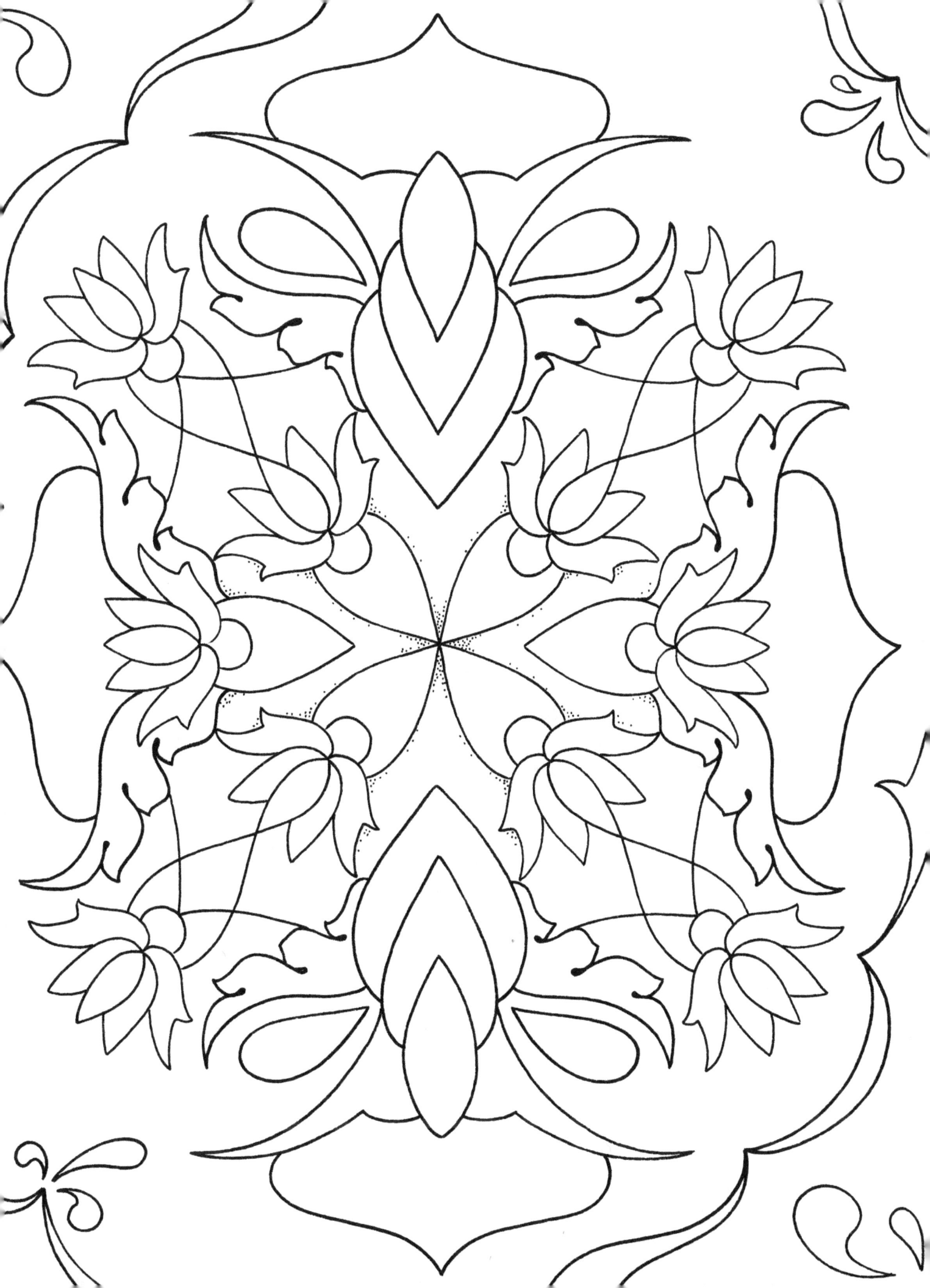

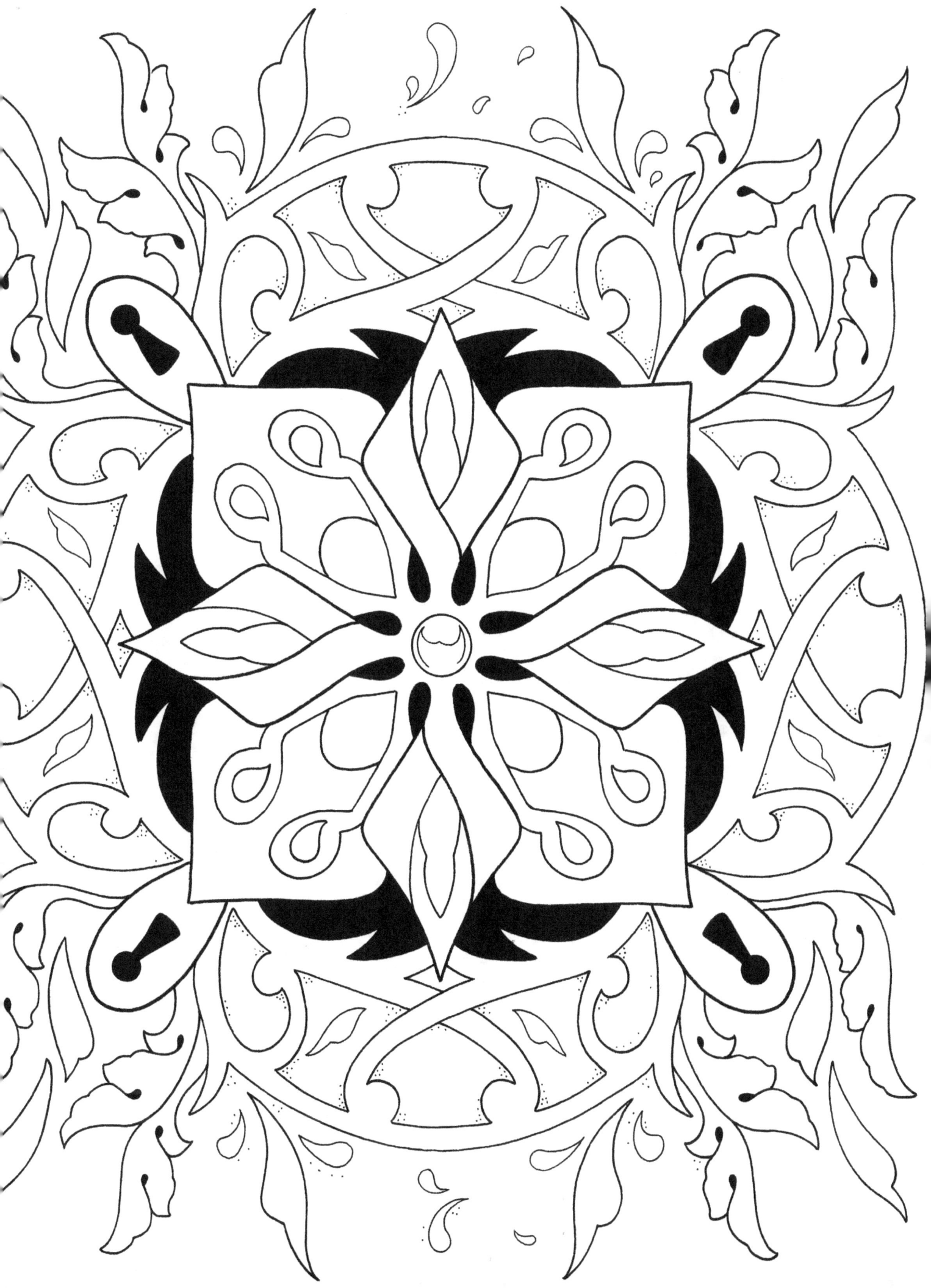

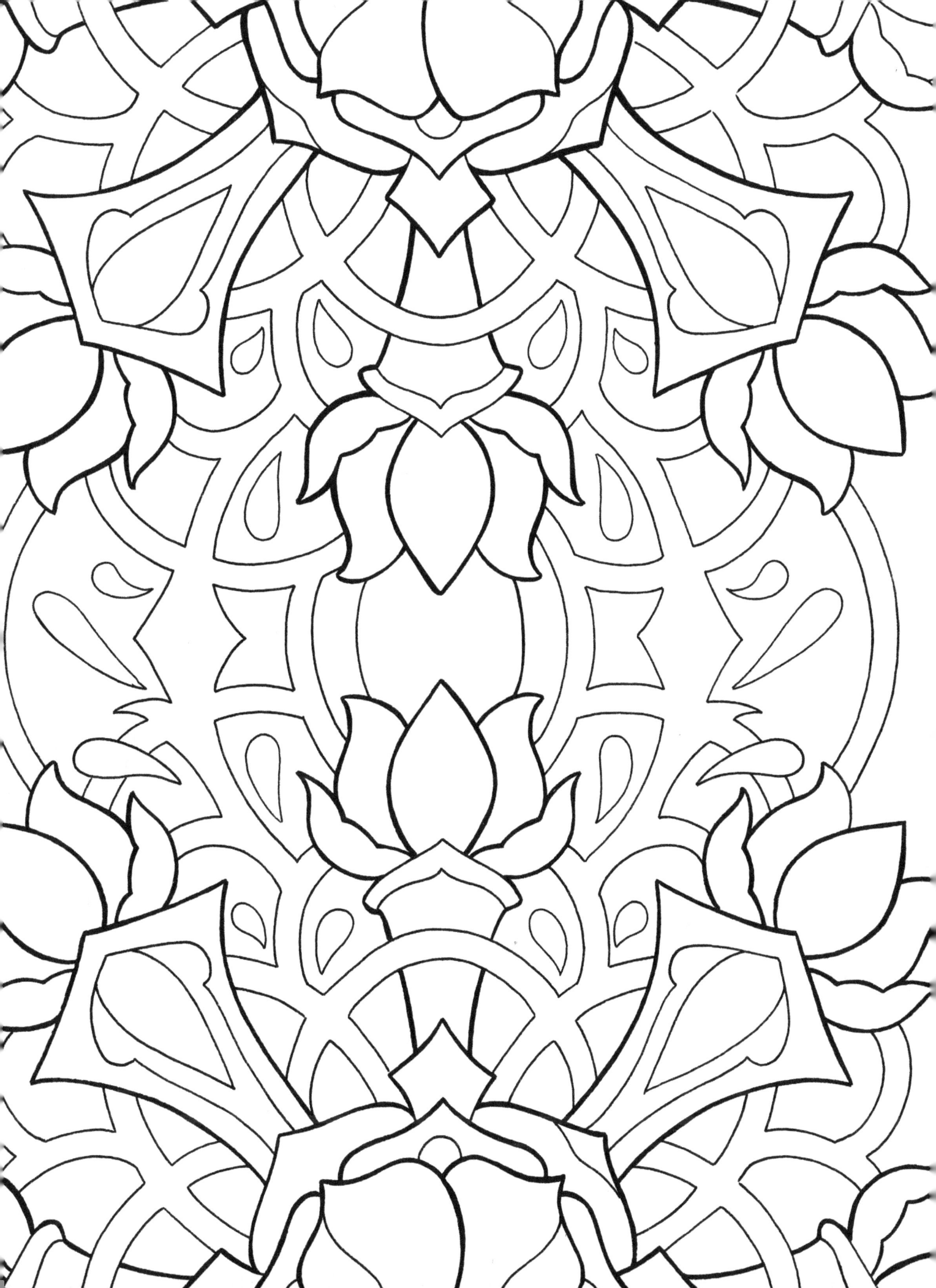

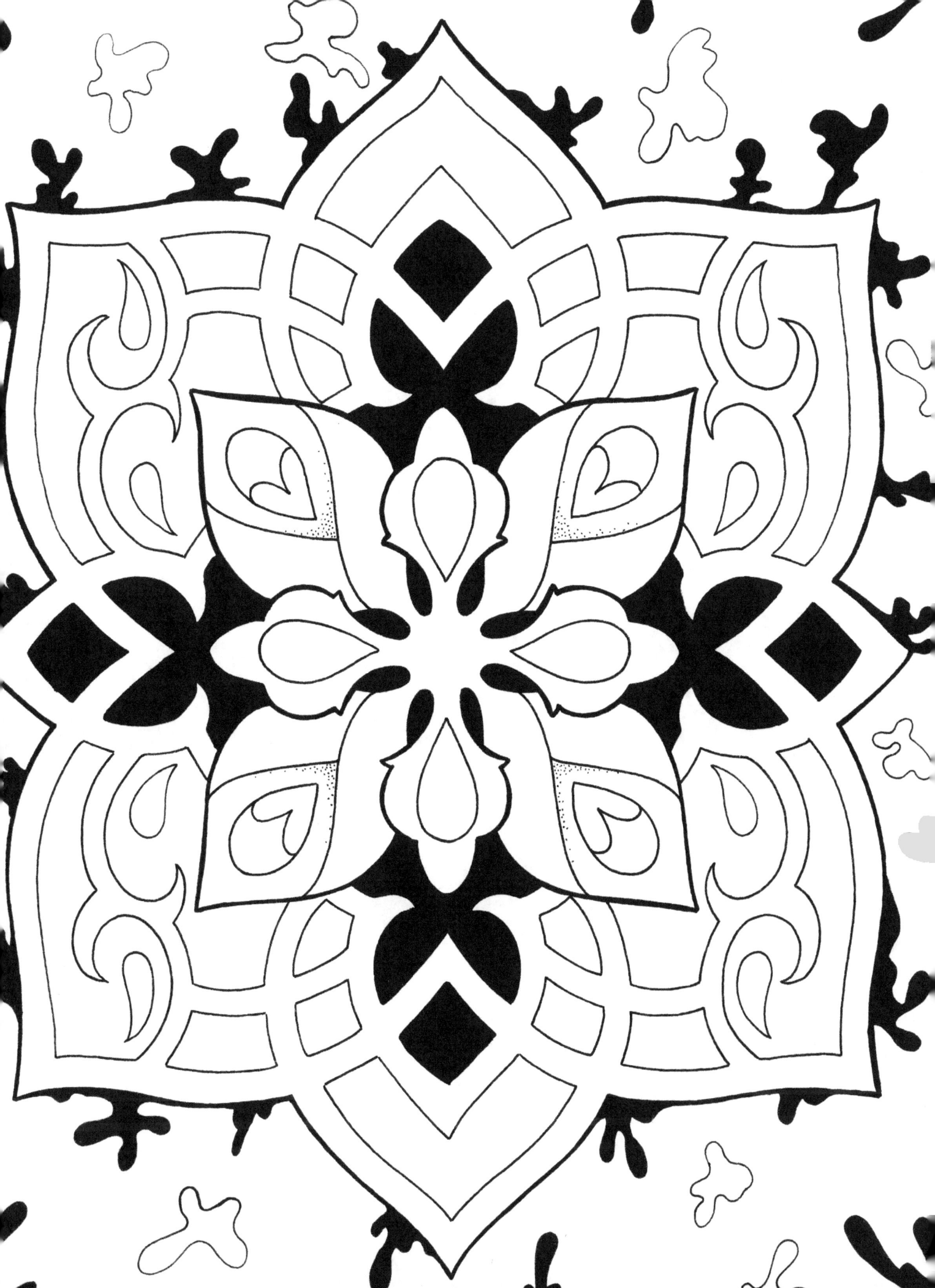

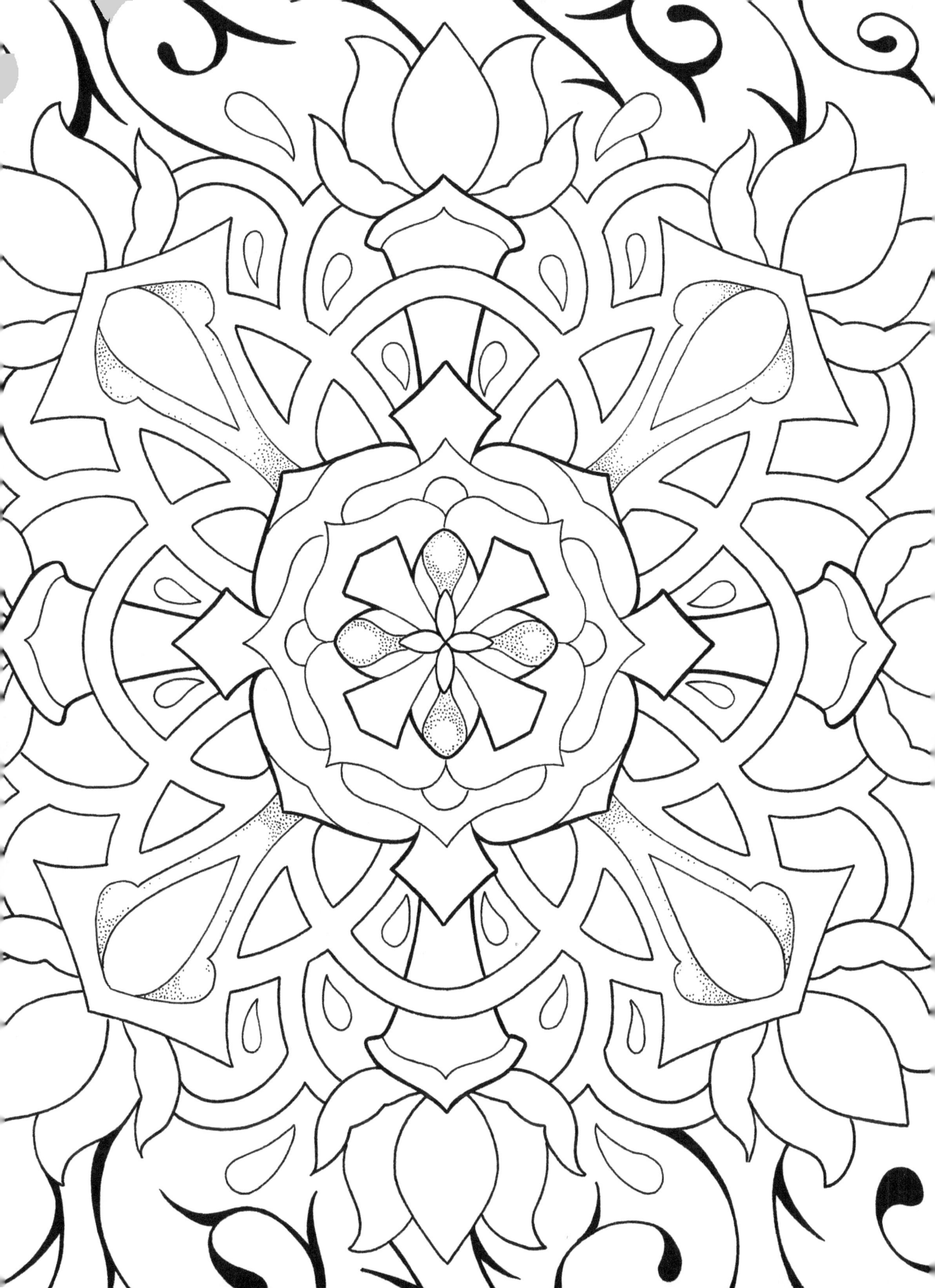

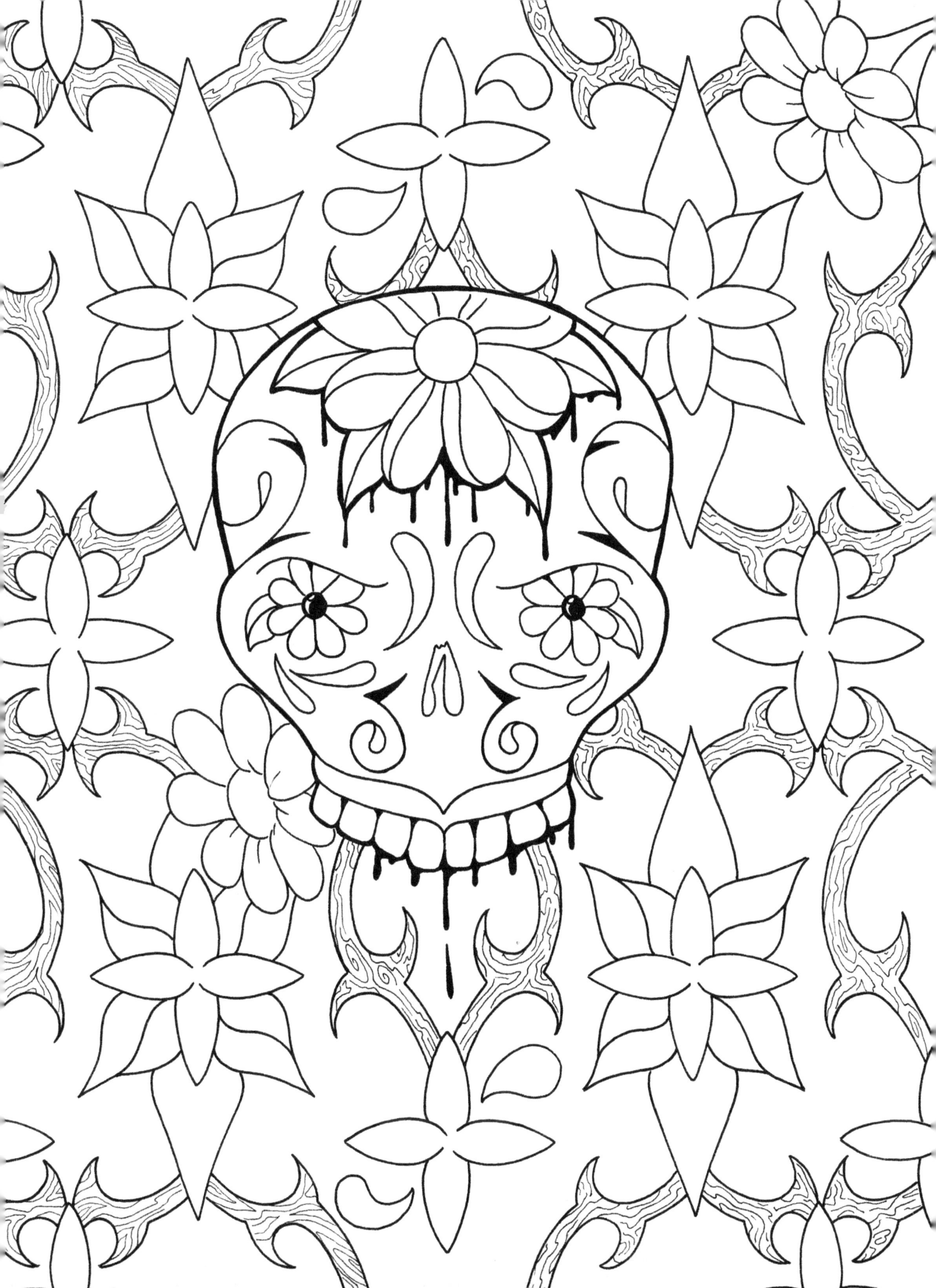

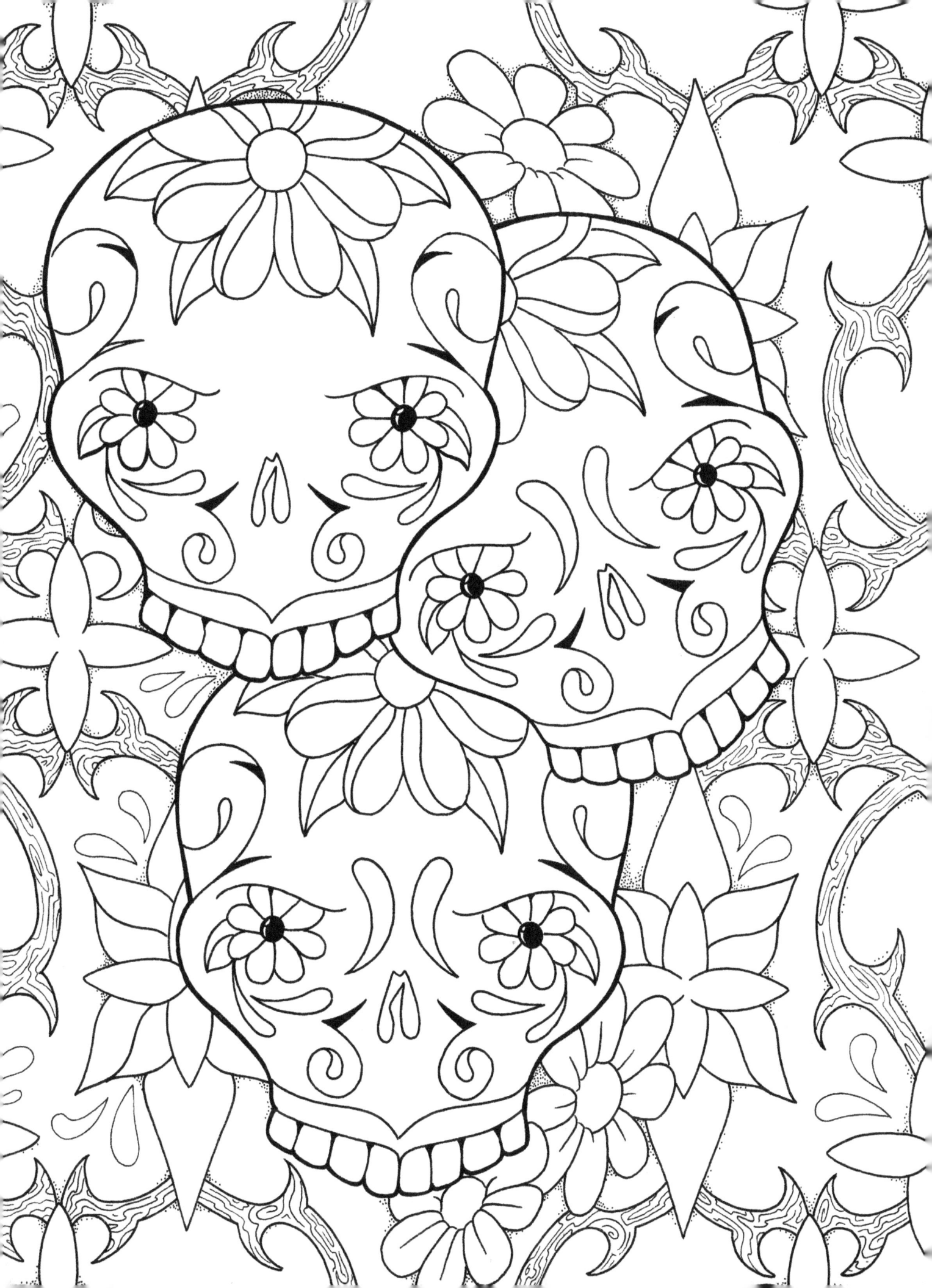

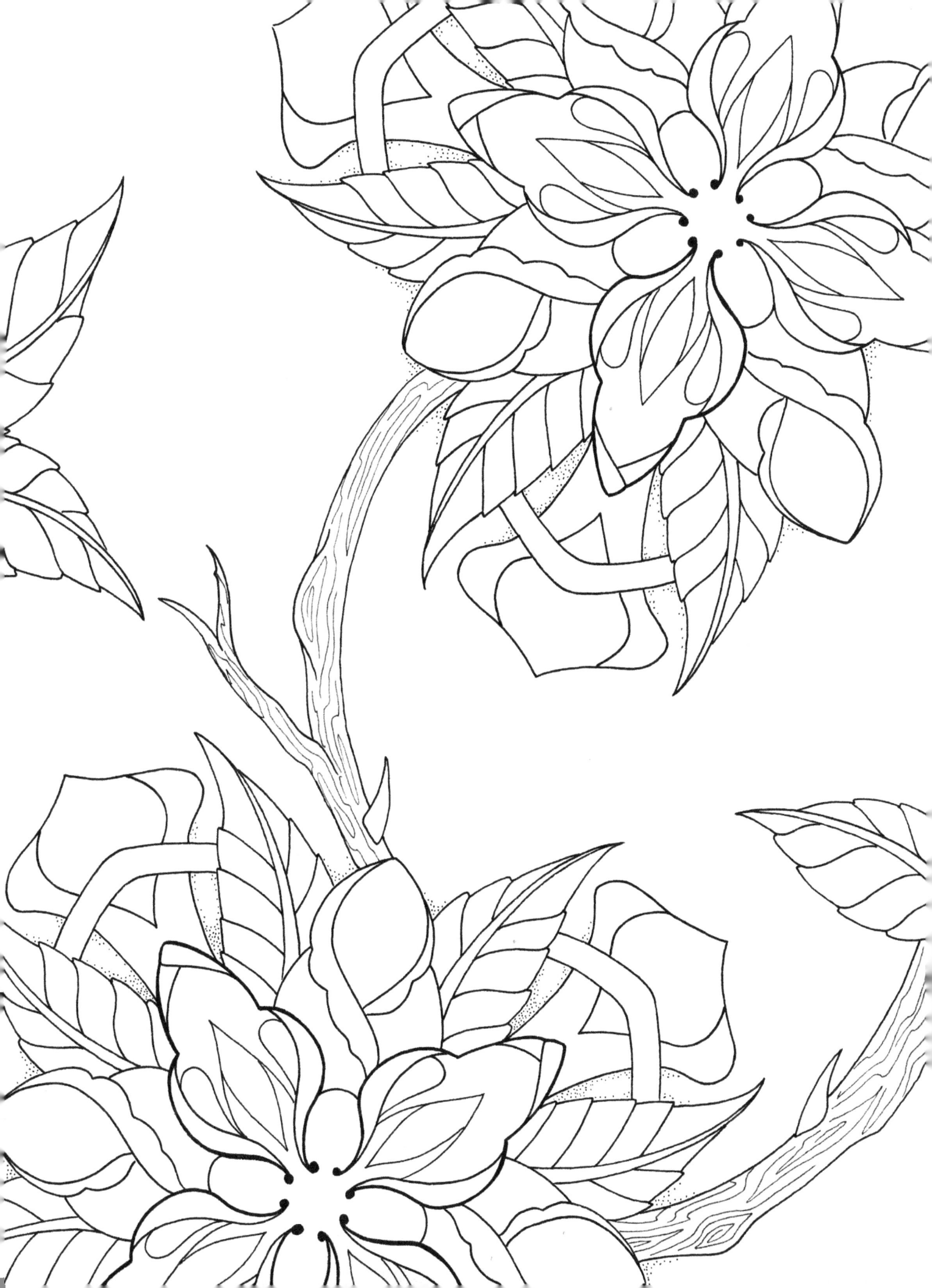

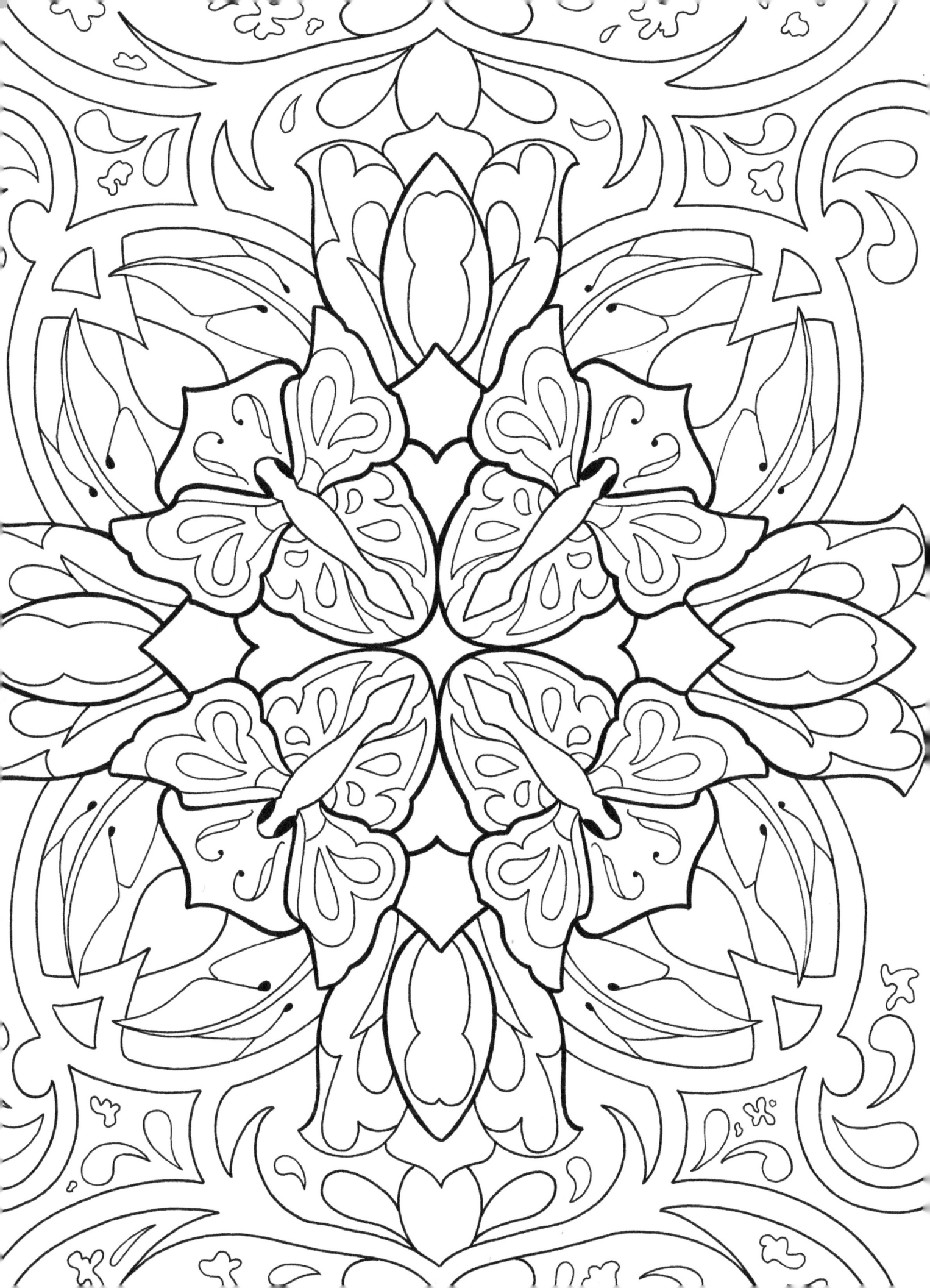

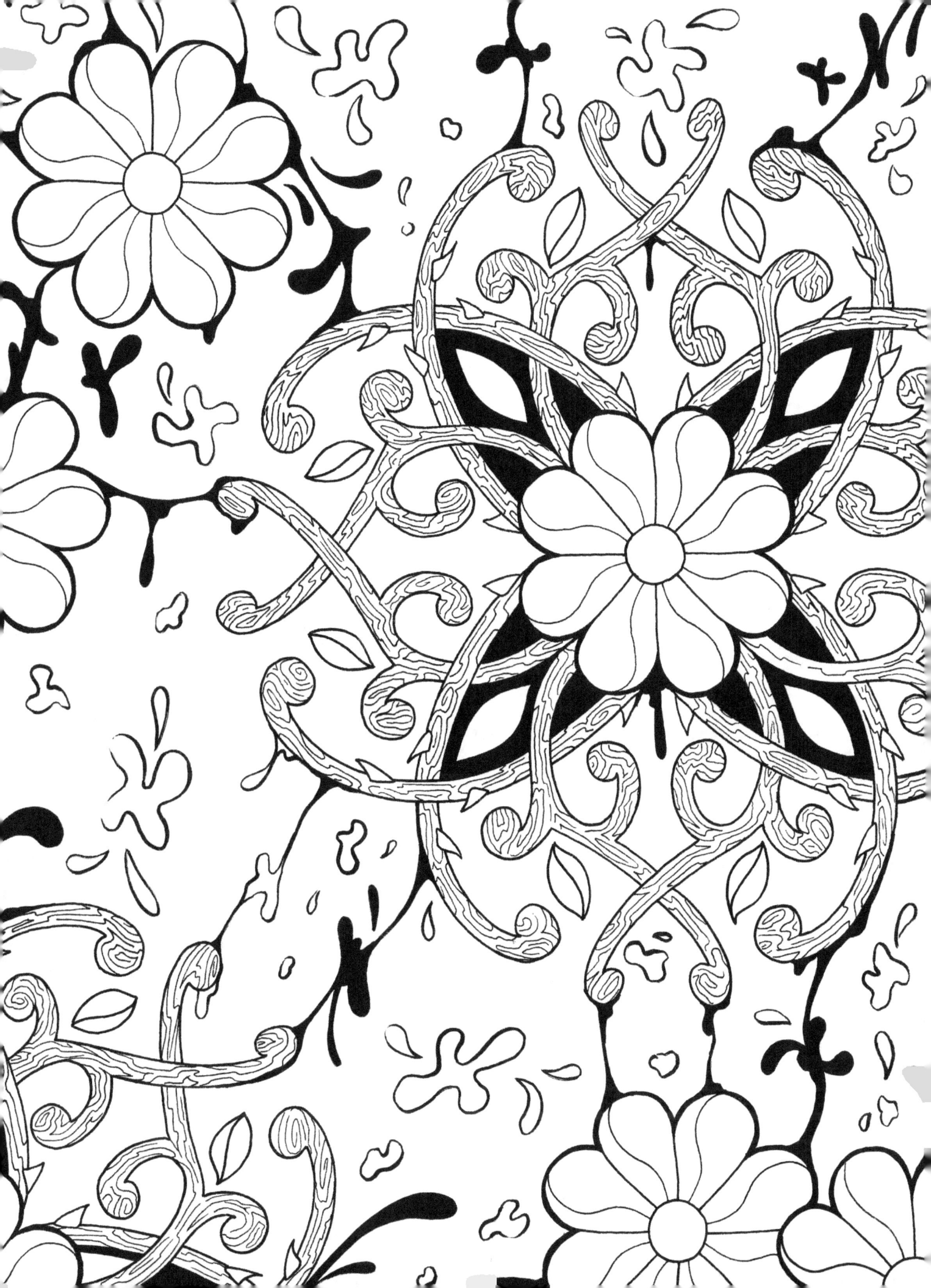

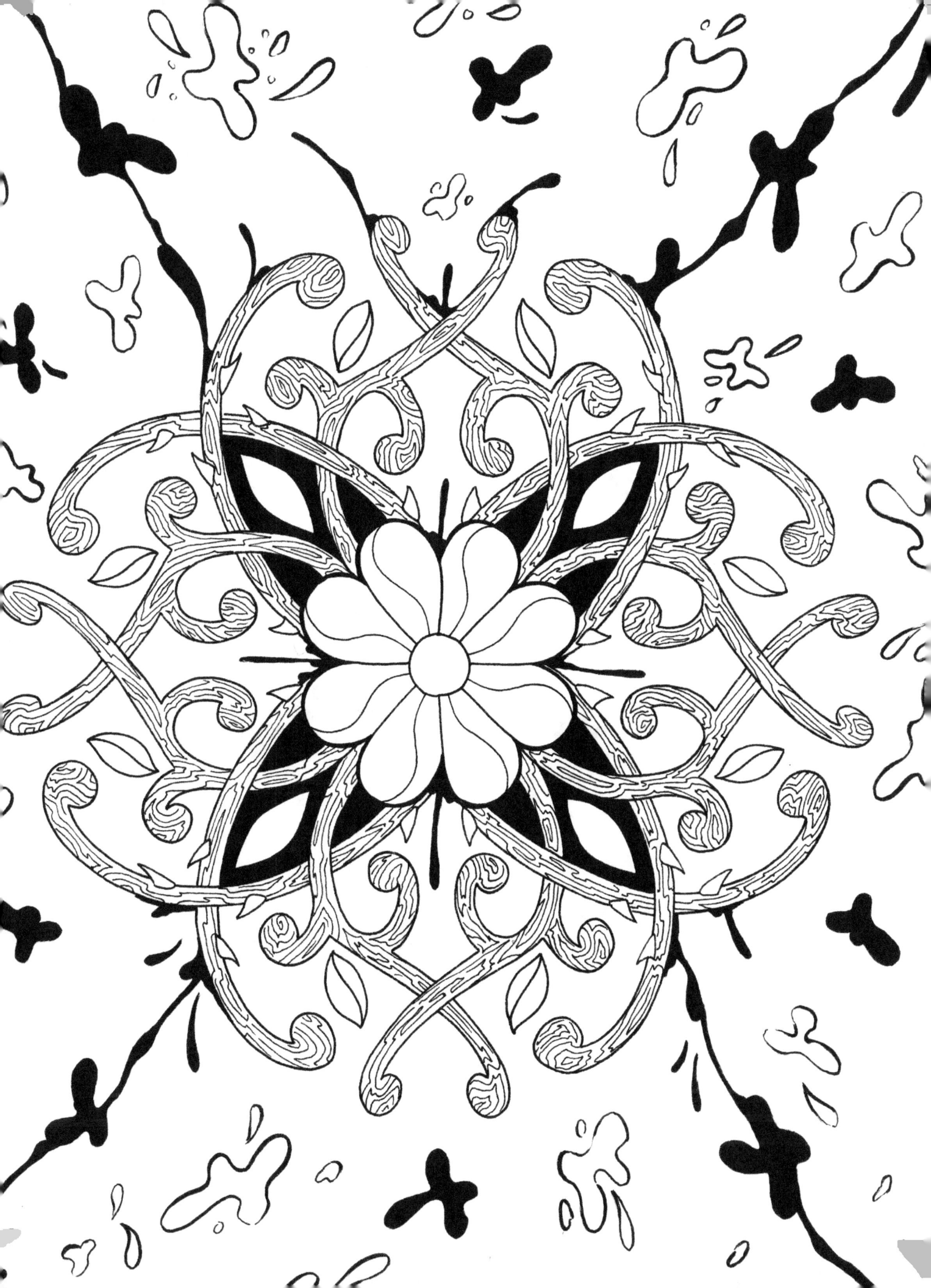

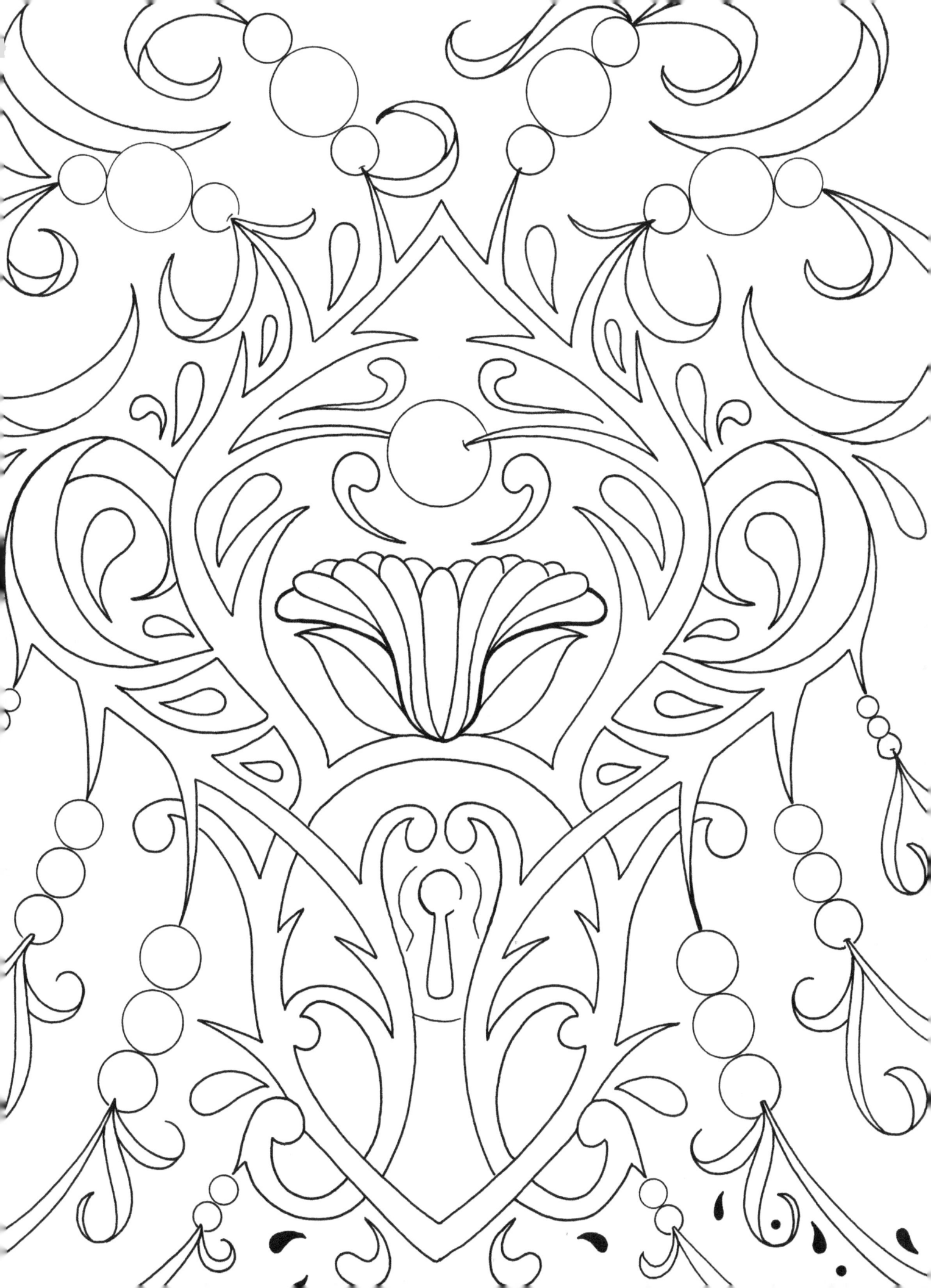

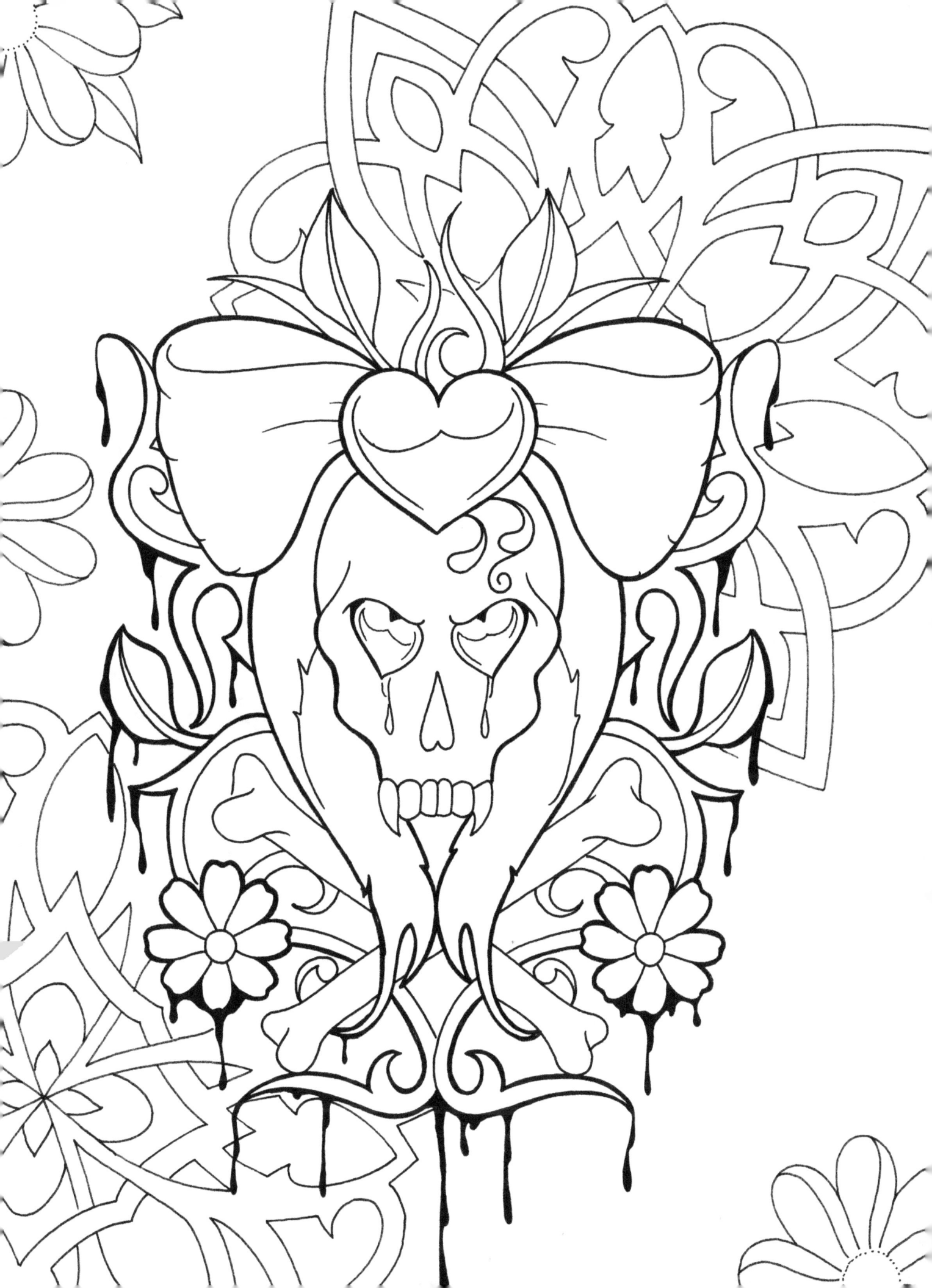

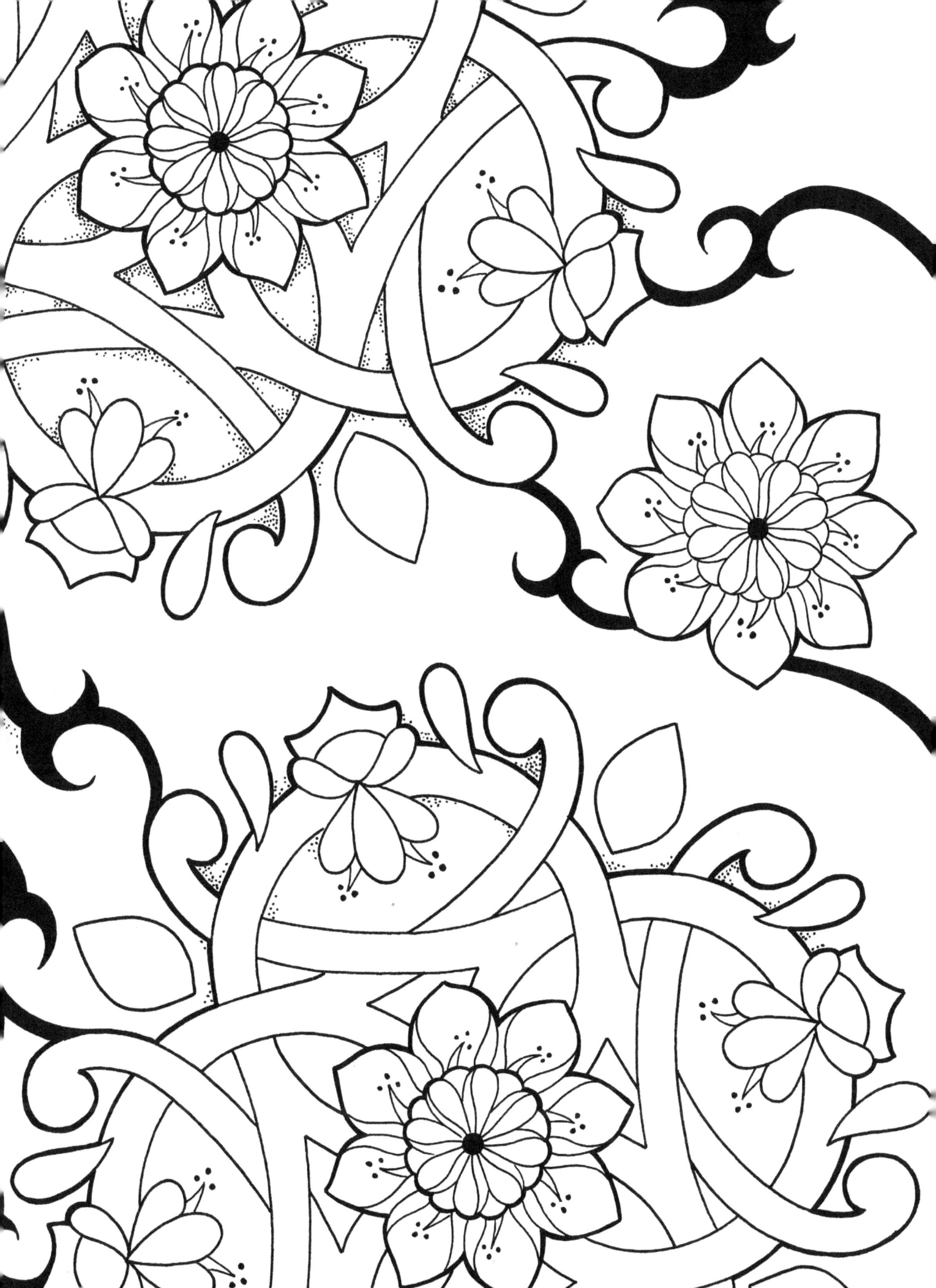

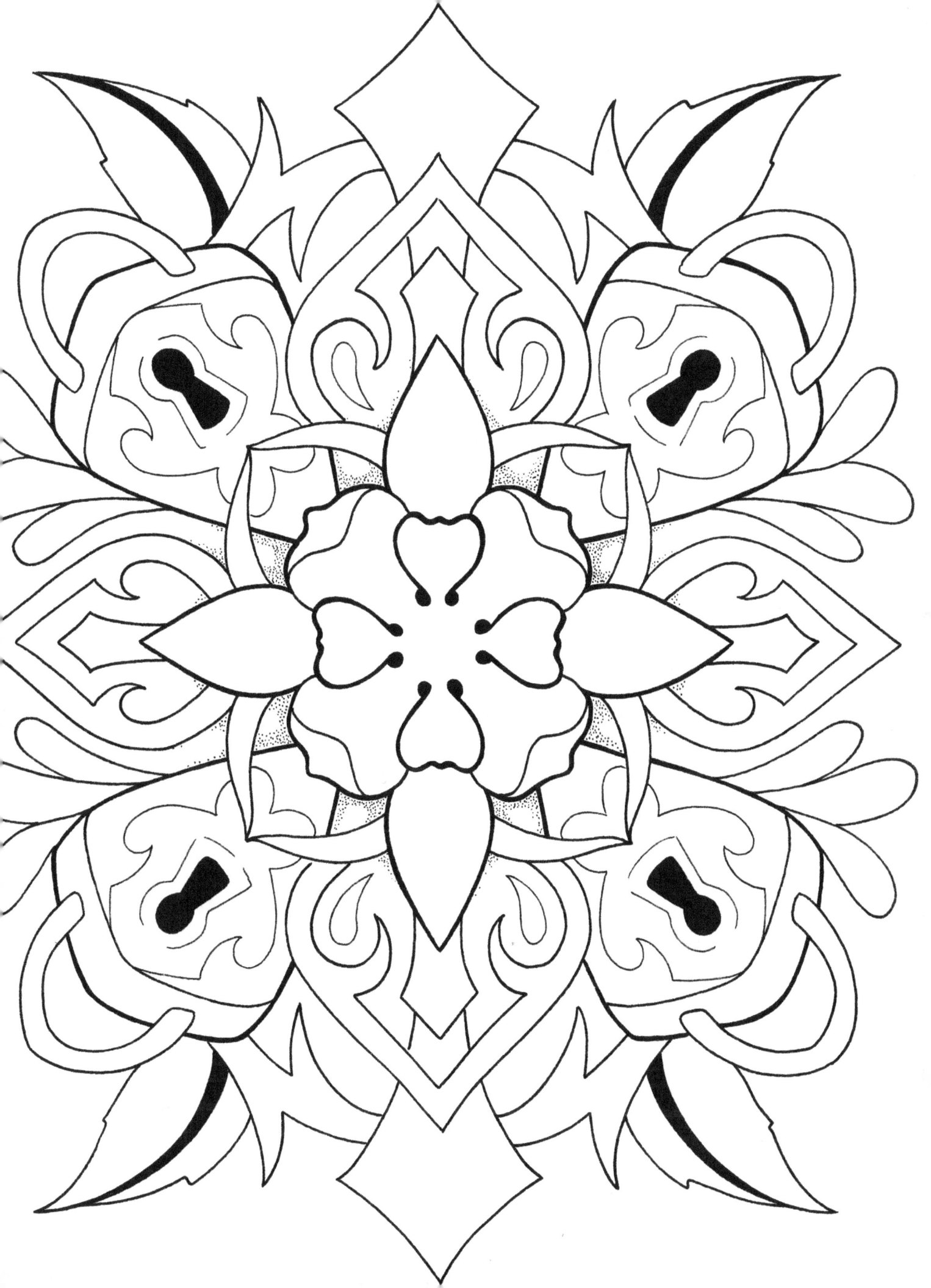

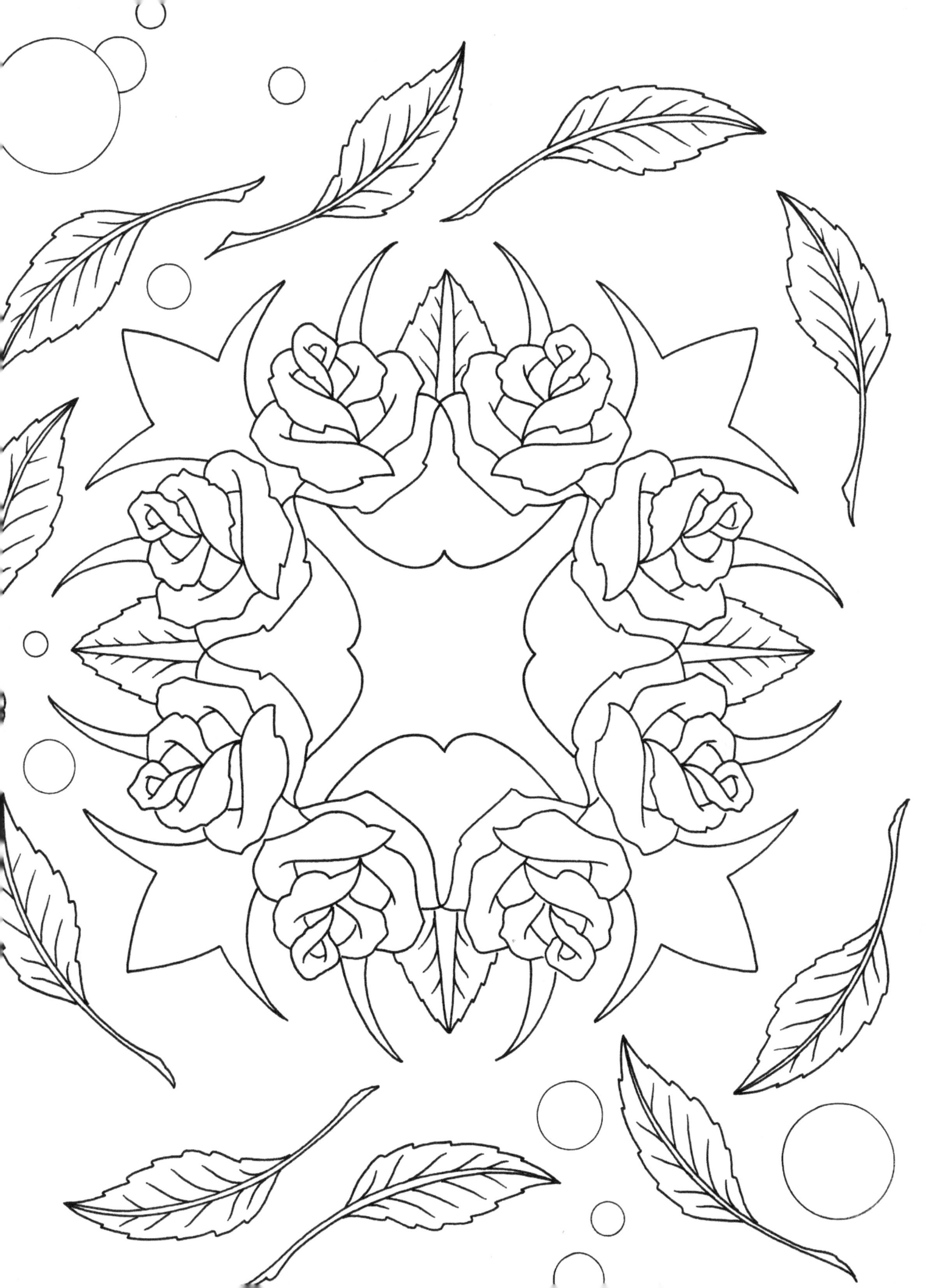

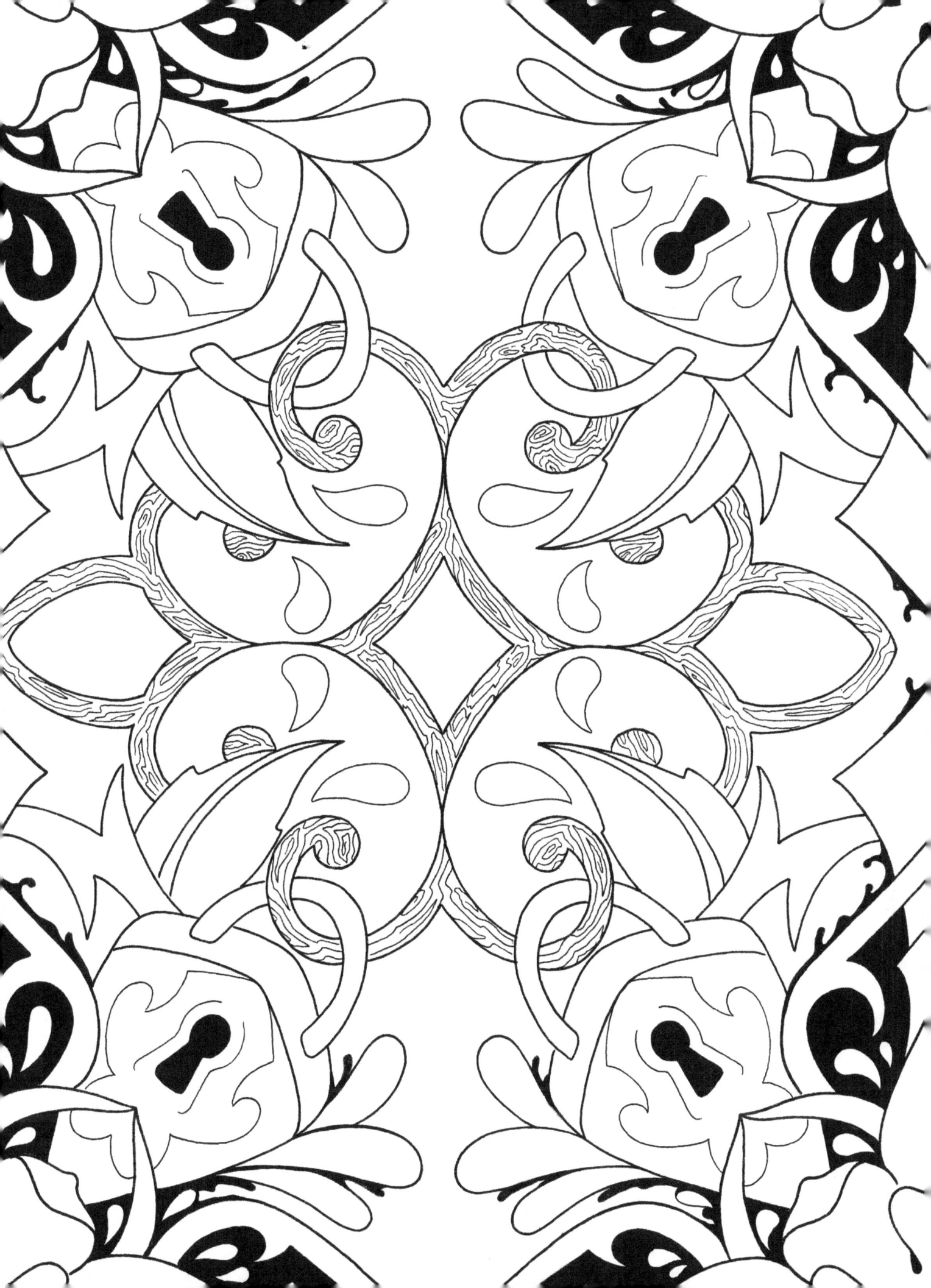

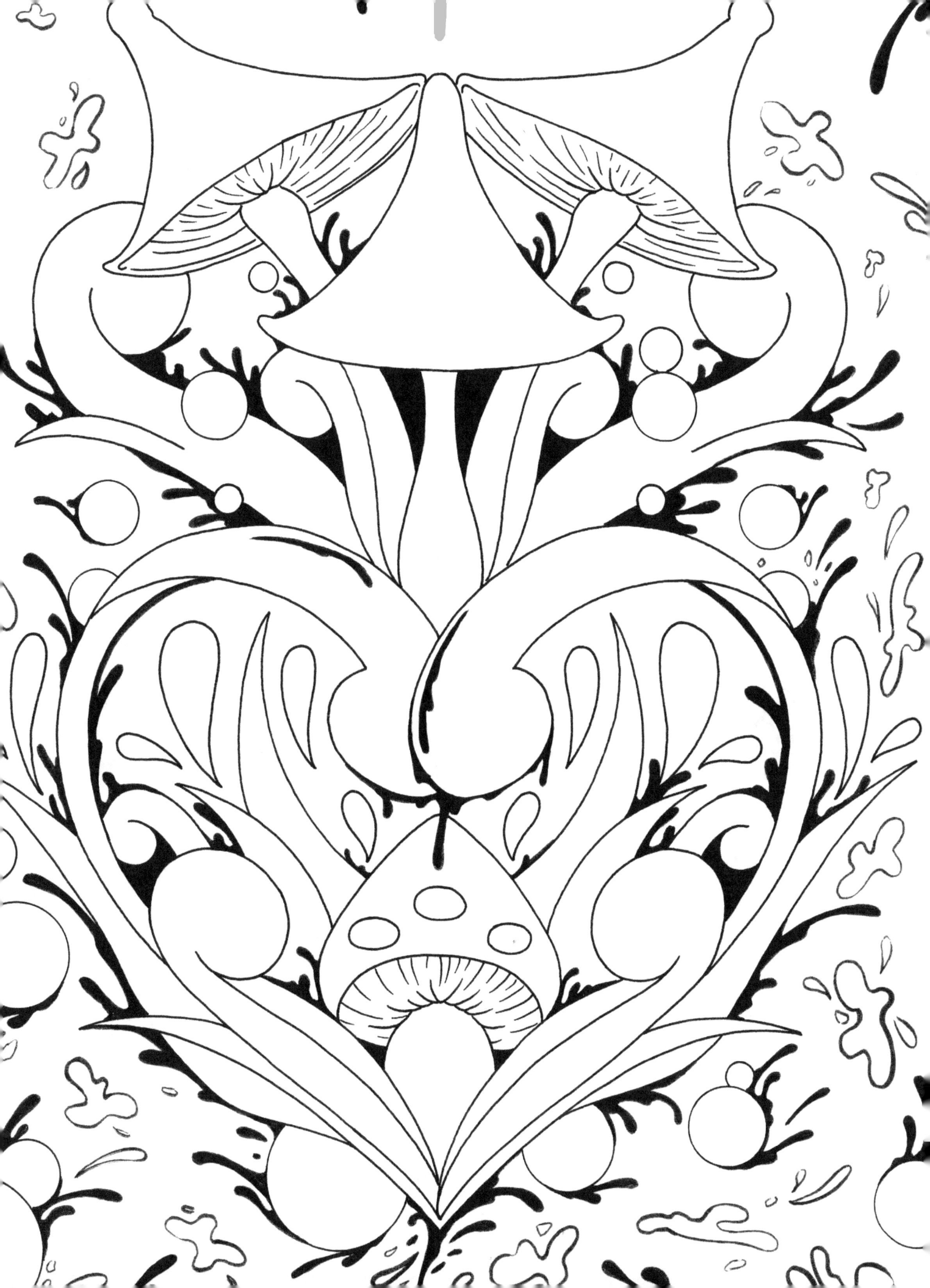

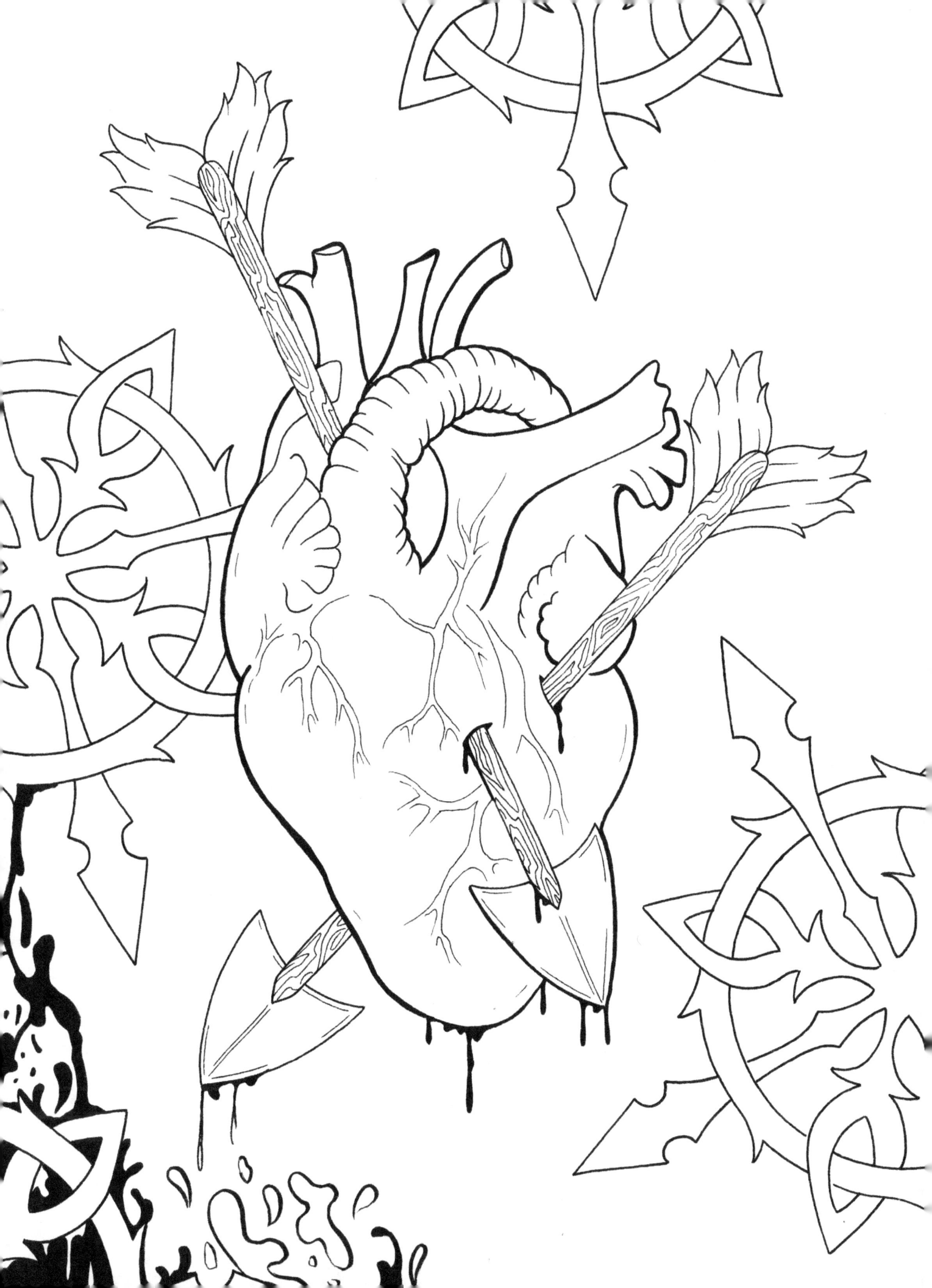

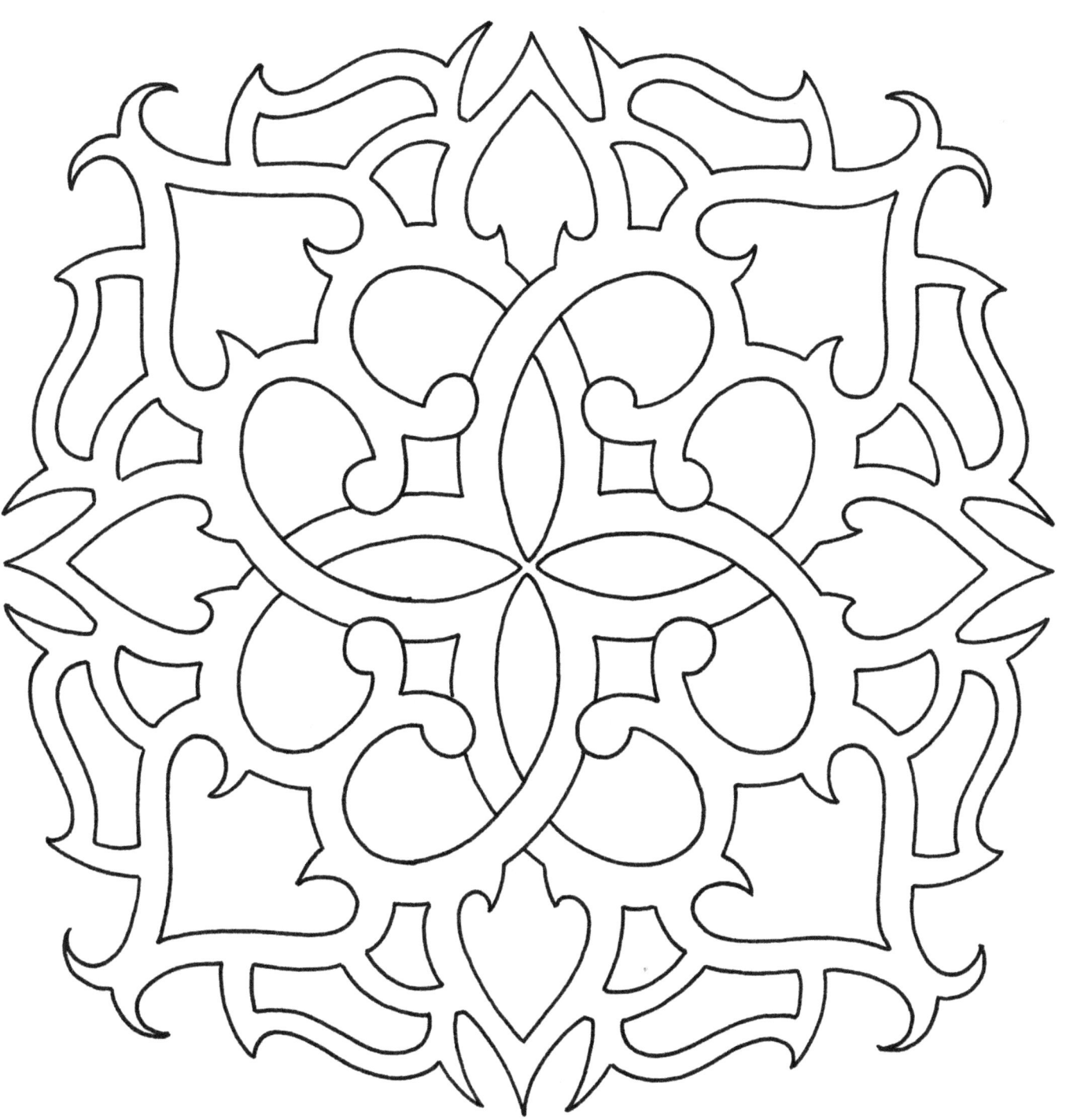

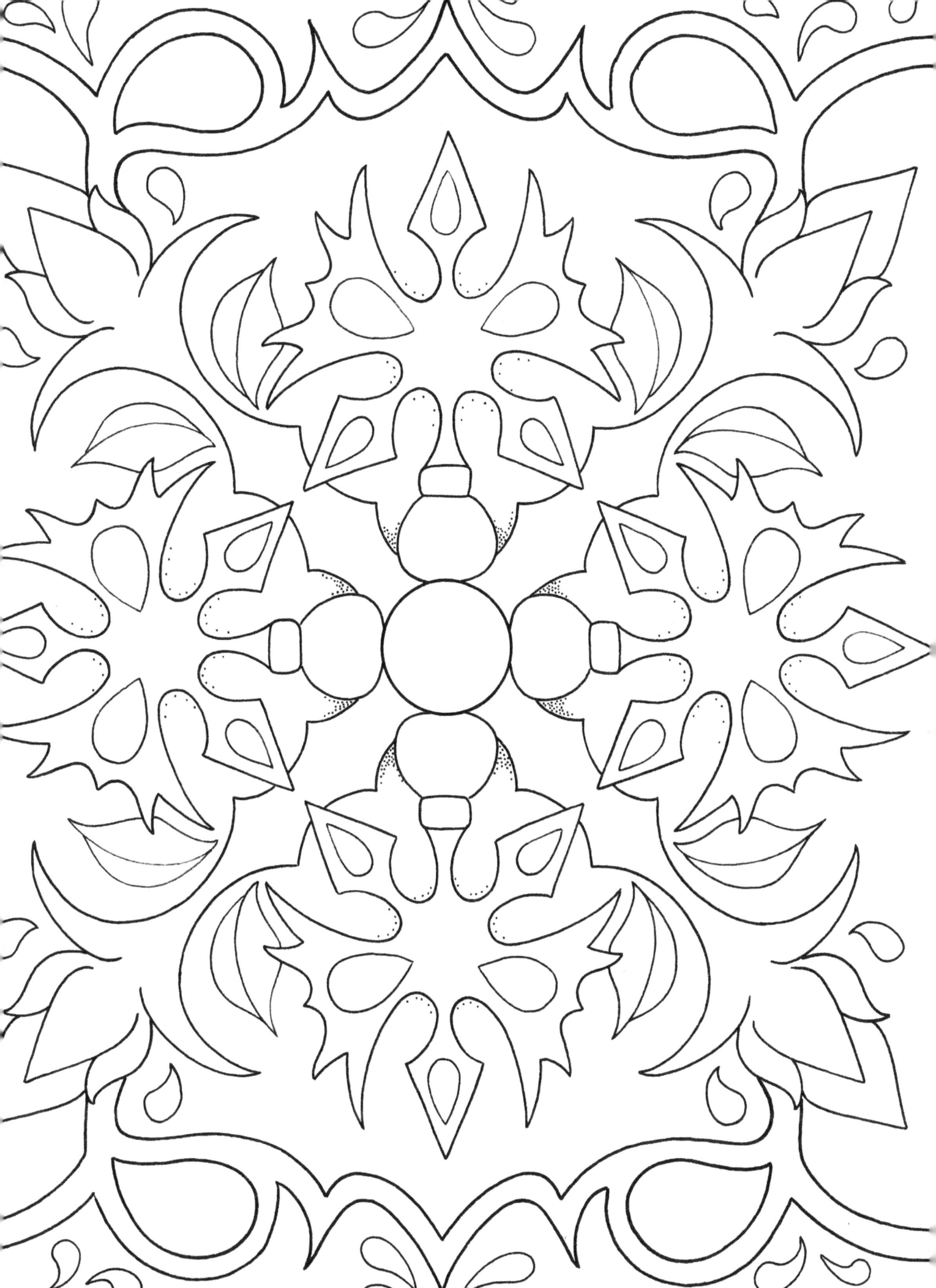

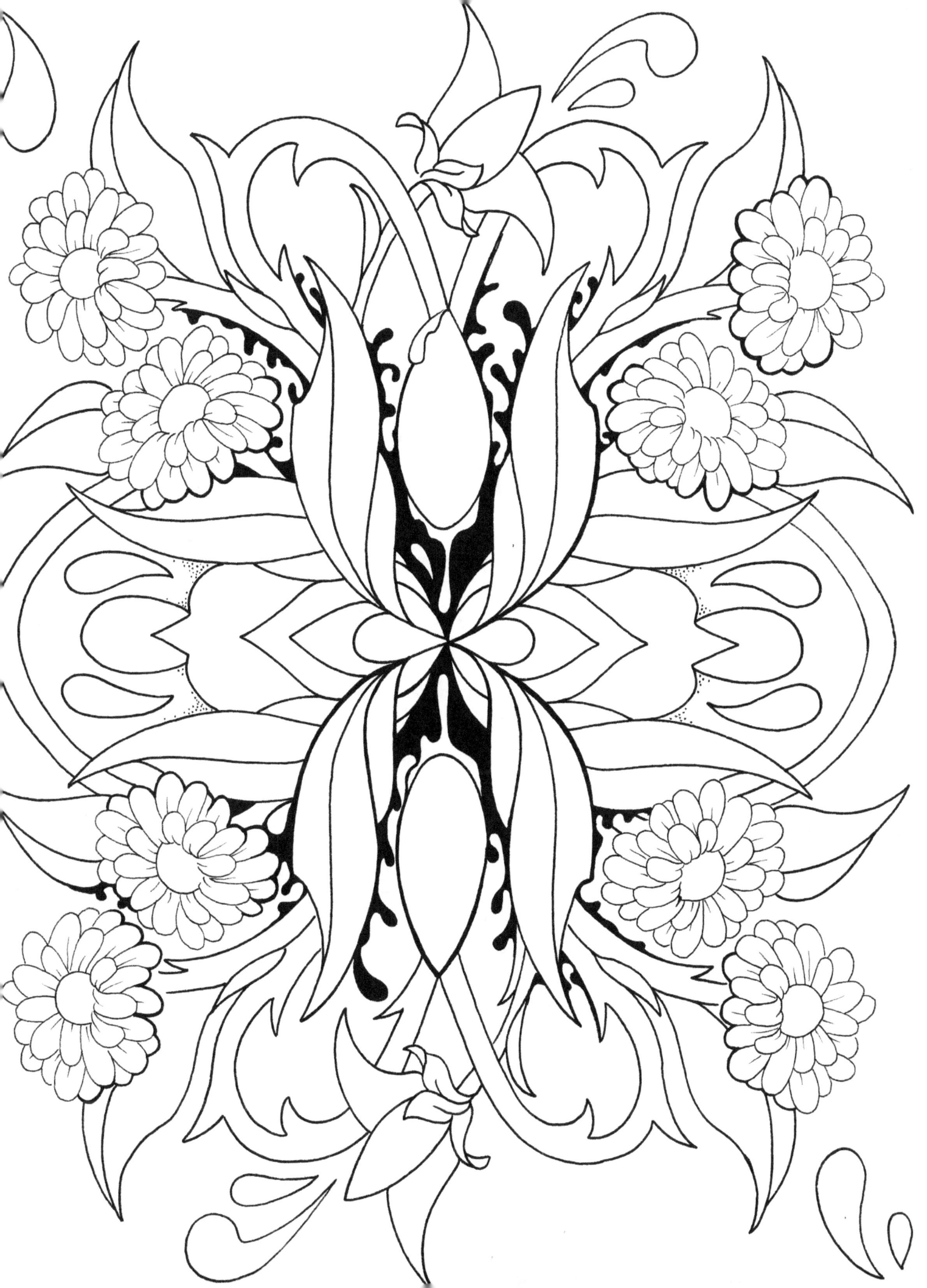

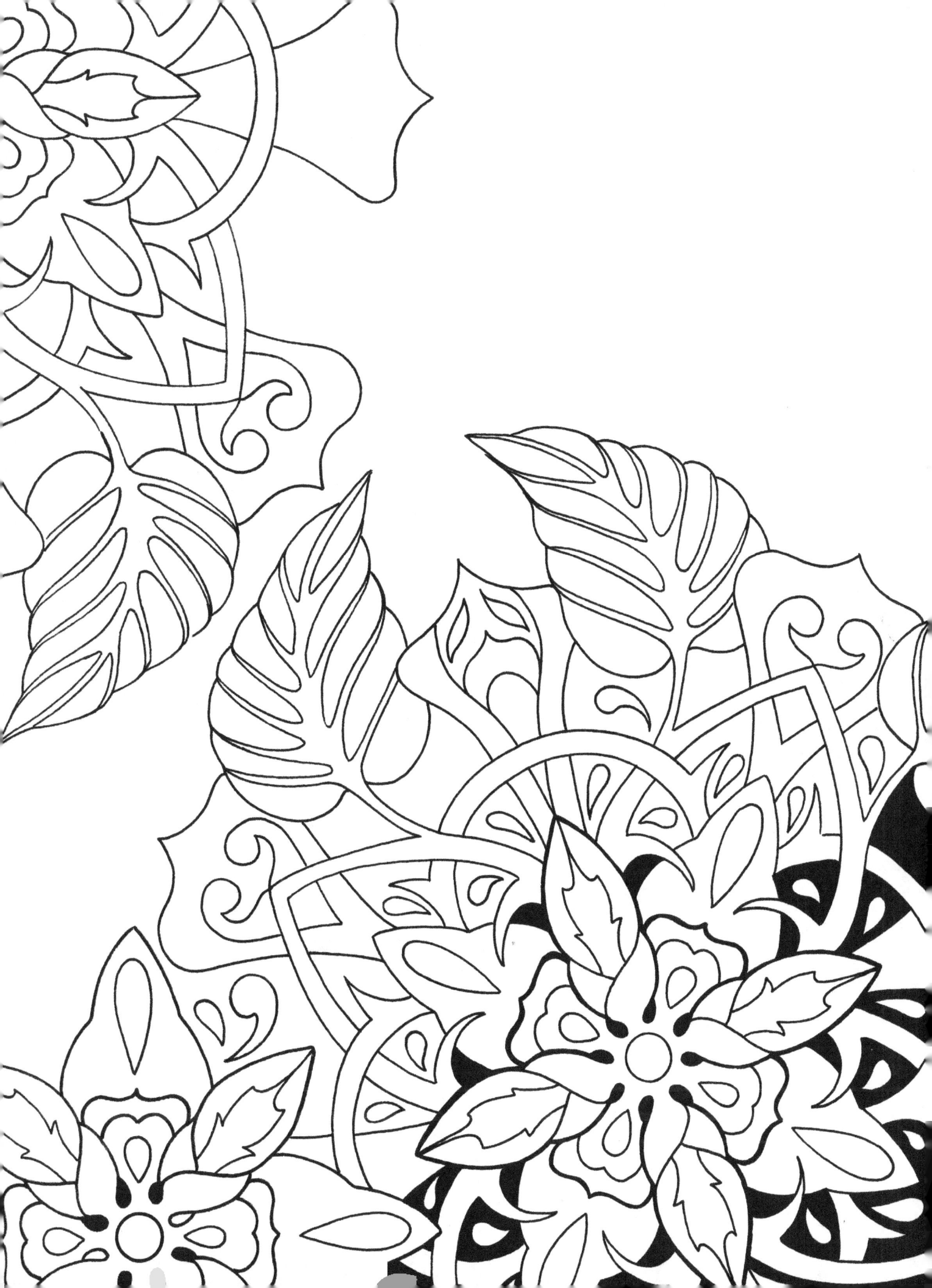

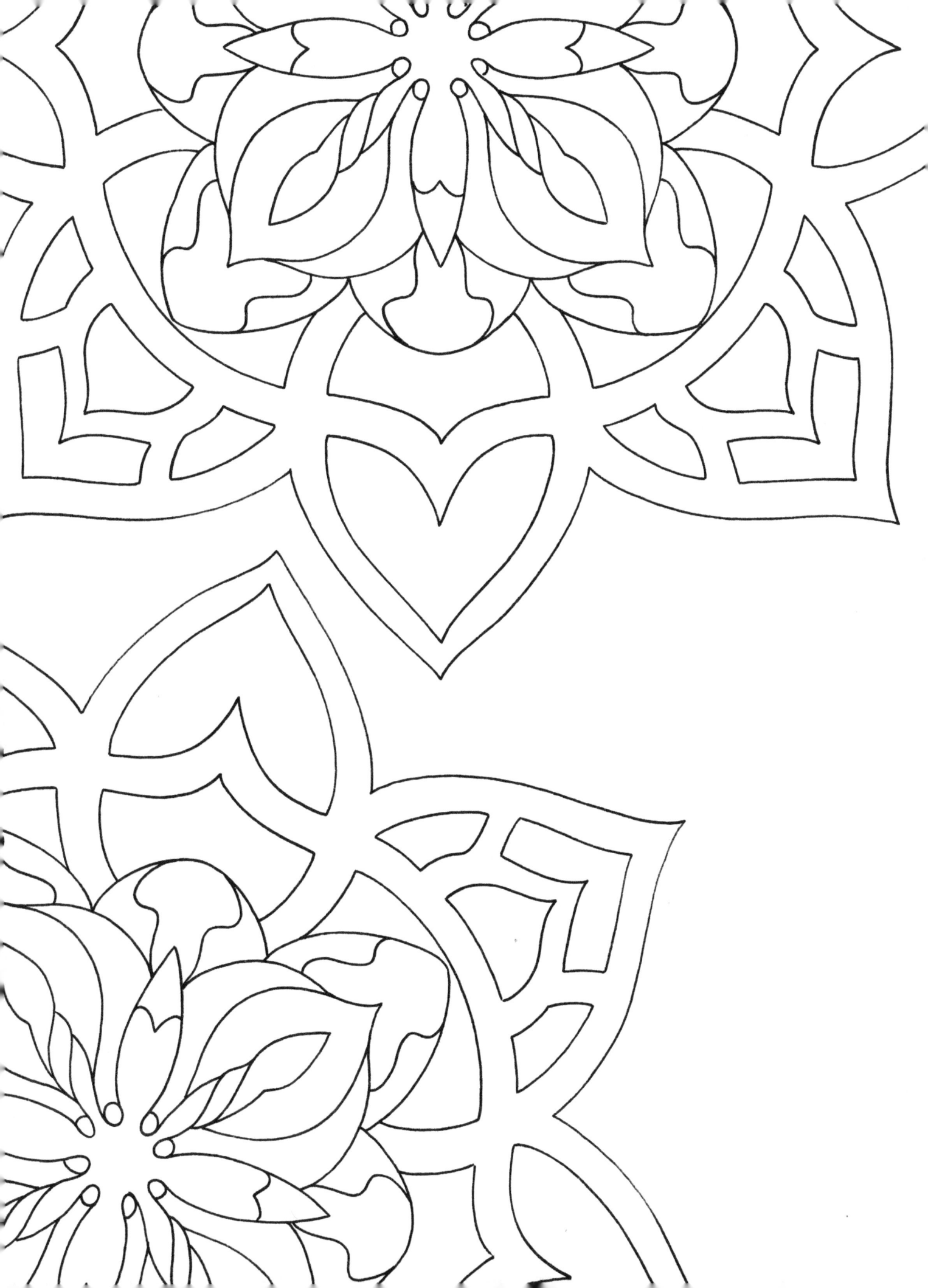

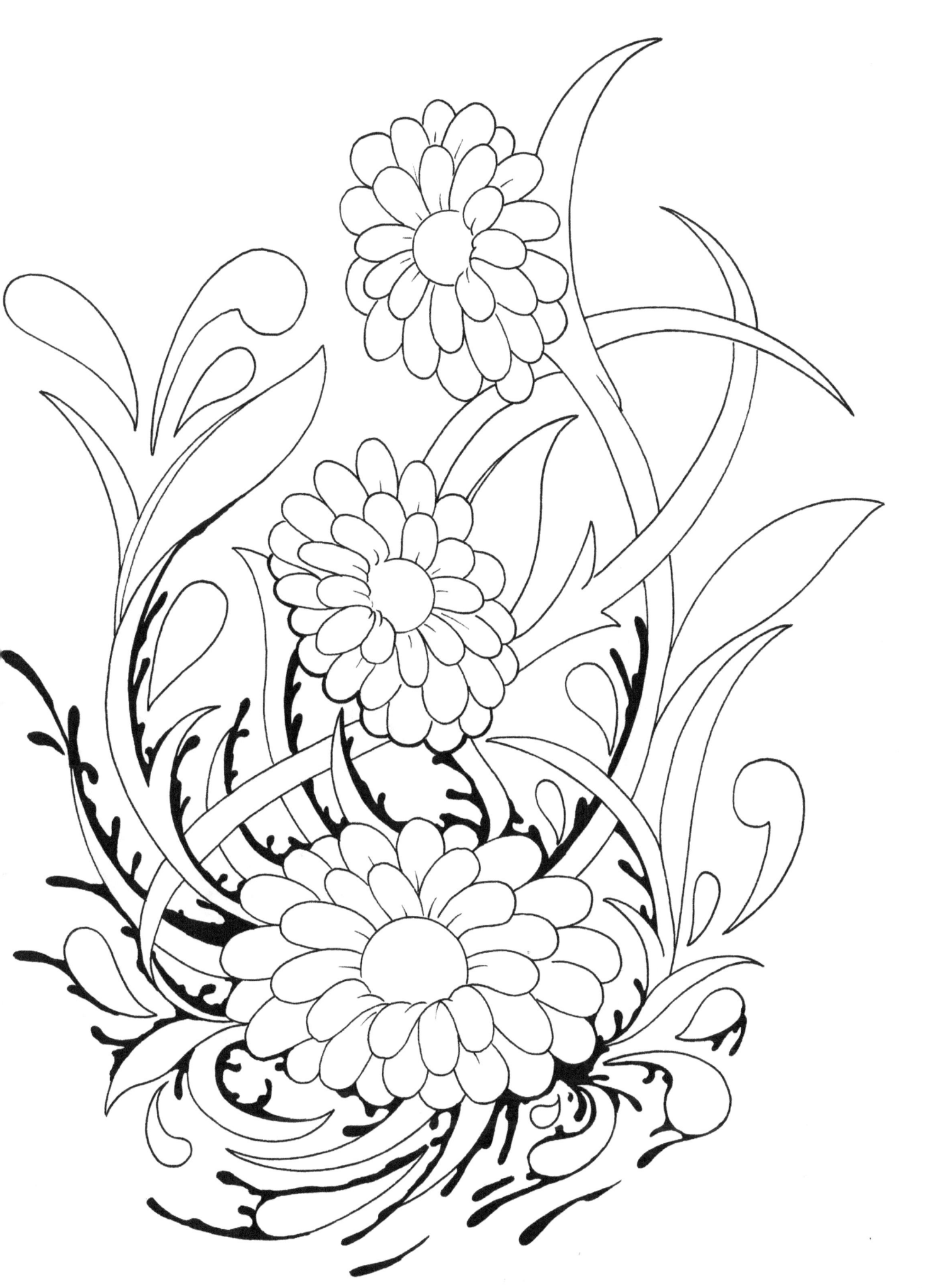

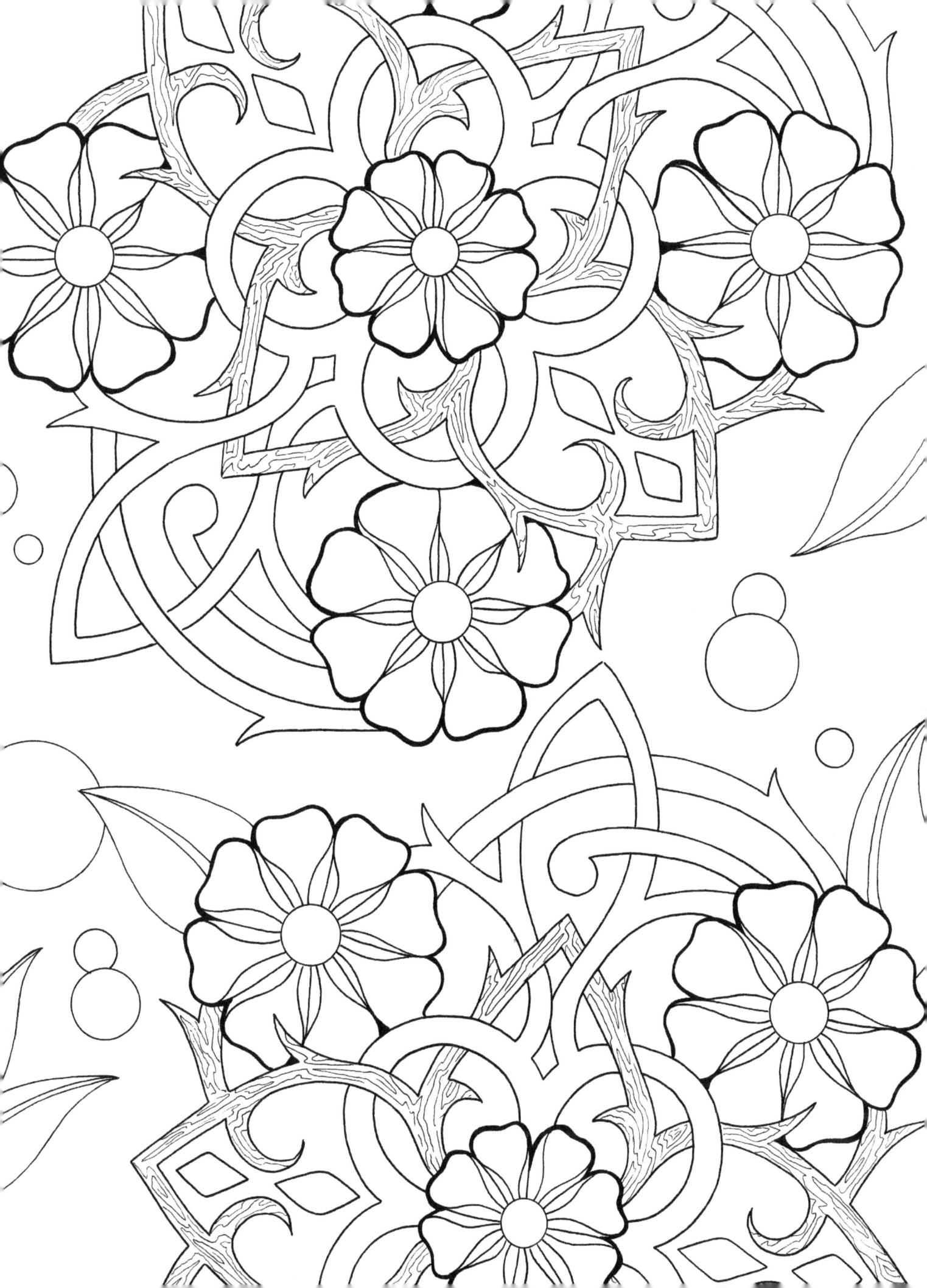

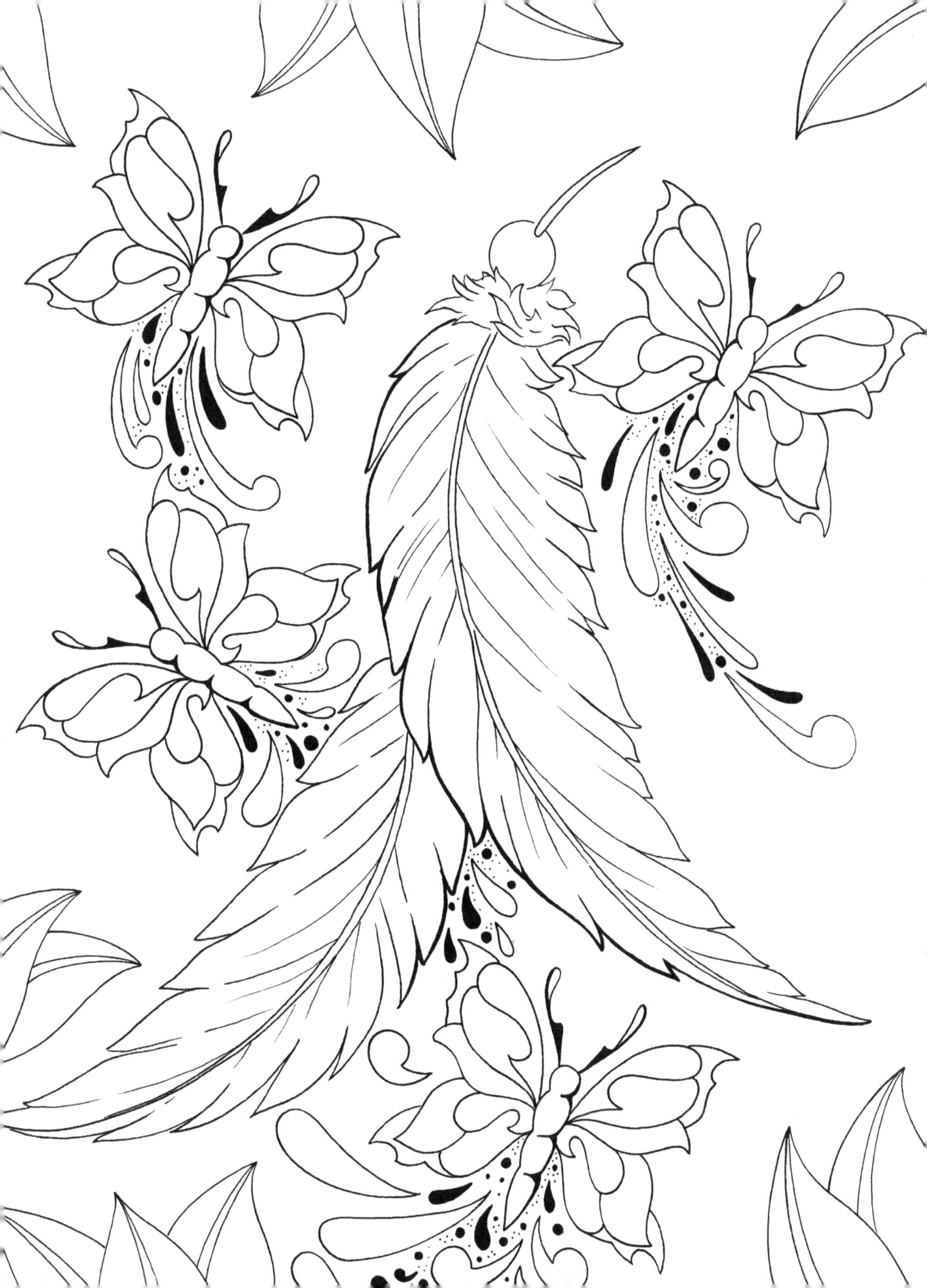

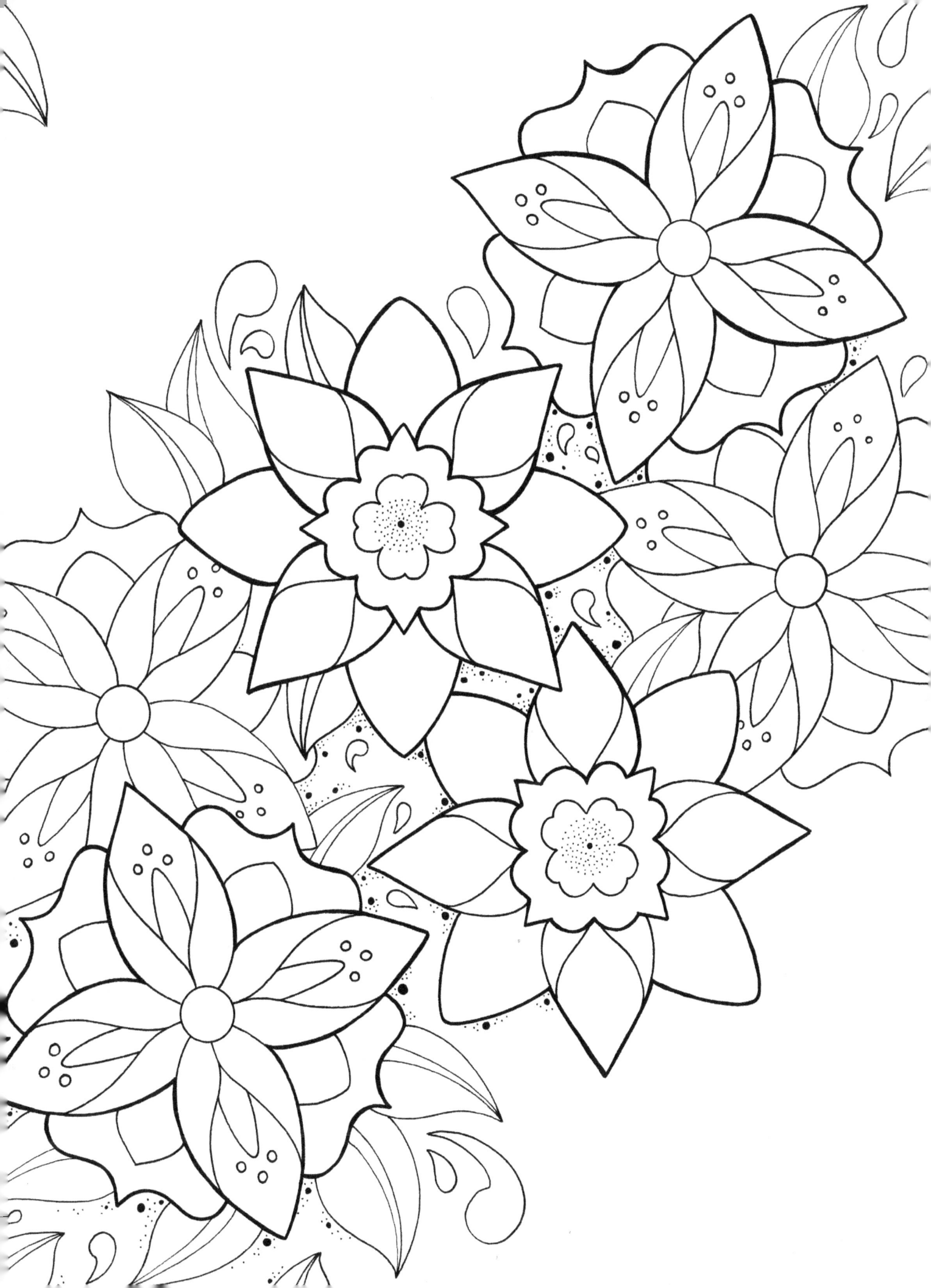

www.ingramcontent.com/pod-product-compliance
Lightning Source LLC
Chambersburg PA
CBHW081012170526
45158CB00010B/3020